To Hazrat, who taught me to love the Beloved and his lovers
May God sanctify your secret
(1938-2015)

The Soliloquy
of the
Full Moon

An Original English Mawlid

محمد رسول الله

The Soliloquy
of the
Full Moon

An Original English Mawlid

Noor-Un-Nisaa Yusuf

Nur al-Habib
Productions

Copyright © 2015 Nur al-Habib Productions www.nuralhabib.com

All rights are reserved. No part of this publication may be reproduced, stored in a retrieval system or transmitted in any form or by any means, electronic, mechanical or otherwise, without prior permission of the publishers.

Title: The Soliloquy of the Full Moon
Subtitle: An Original English Mawlid
Author: Noor-Un-Nisaa Yusuf
Publisher: Nur al-Habib Productions
First Edition: December 2015 / Rabi' al-Awwal 1437

ISBN 978-0-9934979-0-2. Hardback.
1st Edition
A catalogue record for this book is available from the British Library

All Qasida lyrics and melodies by Talib al-Habib
Cover Design: Qutaiba Al-Mahawili, Andromeda Lights

⸺ TABLE *of* CONTENTS ⸺

A Sonnet of Gratitude	9
Foreword	11
Preface: the History of Mawlid	13
Navigating Poetry and Recital	17
Author's Introduction	21
The Soliloquy of the Full Moon	25
Exordium	27
Qasida: the Days of God	28
The Soliloquy Refrain	31
Prologue	33
I. The Beautiful Names	37
II. The Prayer of Ibrahim	41
Qasida: the Lordly Lineage	44
III. The Lineage of the Prophet	47
IV. The Year of the Elephant	51
V. The Blessed Birth	55
Qasida: In the Still of the Night	59
VI. The Nursing of the Prophet	63
VII. Revelations	67
VIII. The Night Journey	73
IX. The Ascension	79
Qasida: The Ascension	85
X. A Pen Portrait	87
Qasida: Hilyat al-Nabi	91
XI. His Exalted Character	93
Qasida: O You to Whom the Bird Complained	97
XII. Epilogue	101
Appendix: Love's Harvest	105

ACKNOWLEDGEMENT
A Sonnet of Gratitude

MAY every word herein to Him be raised,
And thankfulness accorded in full breadth
To all who helped this work's completion. May,
In God's transcendent court, their names be read:

The Winter Shaykh for words of warm support;
The Ward of manuscripts for close critique;
The Lordly teacher who my teacher taught;
The Sayyid for confirming it *sahih*.

Li'l-umm, wa'l-ab, wa'l-ukht wa'l-hirratayn,
And to the Fellowship Insep'rable,
To family – too numerous to name –
My love to all of them for their good will.

And unto Kazi, Muhyi al-Din Ghulam,
The Prophet – peace on him – and Al-Rahman.

FOREWORD
On the First Traditional English Mawlid

IN GOD'S NAME, the Infinitely Good, the Most Merciful. All praise is for Allah, who bestowed upon our Master Adam ﷺ knowledge of the names of all things, and upon his progeny the gifts of intellect and speech. Peace and blessings be upon our Master Muhammad, the last of His Emissaries – and the foremost of them – who while being himself the most eloquent of mankind, also informed us in a Tradition that his panegyric poet Hassan ibn Thabit ﷺ was 'aided by angelic inspiration.'

In keeping with the Divine injunction to show thankfulness for blessings received, Muslim communities in many lands have a long-standing tradition of gathering to celebrate the arrival of the one sent as a mercy to the entire universe, may Allah exalt and preserve him. Alhamdulillah, there exists a large body of literary works inspired by the desire to raise the level of knowledge and love among those participating in such events, and of those seeking to brighten their hearts and free them of worldly cares at any time or place the Divine Compassion may determine.

Up to now, the only such works available in English have been translations from Arabic, Urdu, Turkish, and other languages spoken chiefly by Muslims. All these have their merits, and may Allah reward all those who have expended of their talent and efforts in producing such works in praise of the Best of Mankind, such as the Mawlids of

THE SOLILOQUY OF THE FULL MOON

Süleyman Çelebi, Imam Barzanji, Habib 'Umar and many others.

Allah be praised, our young sister Noor Yusuf has now been inspired to produce a Mawlid in the English language – the first one the present writer has ever seen. Designed for recitation and performance, it is written in both rhyme and metre, following the rules of prosody. This is not to deny the value of encouraging free-form creative writing by young and old alike.

On a different level, however, poetry (especially spiritual poetry) is an art form, a craft that demands sustained hard work and for which good intentions, though essential, are not sufficient. Those who have received the calling may spend a lifetime honing their poetical skills. In mediaeval times it was considered a necessary part of poets' training to memorise thousands of lines of verse by their great predecessors.

In 'The Soliloquy of the Full Moon' we encounter an original and telling poetic concept which reflects the truth that there is nothing in the heavens or the earth that is not praising its Almighty and Omniscient Creator; and that the moon is one of His creations that appears again and again in different aspects of Islam and in the life of every Muslim: the splitting of the moon mentioned in the Qur'an, and Allah Most High swearing therein by the sun and moon; the recording of time through their movements; and many other matters. And Allah Most High knows best.

Noor is a young lady who has grasped both the momentousness of the subject and the need to have high resolve and make maximum effort to produce a work that is worthy of it. May Allah accept this 'Soliloquy' of hers and make it a means for multitudes to draw near to Him through their devotion to His Beloved Emissary ﷺ.

Dr Muhammad Isa Waley
Curator of Islamic Manuscripts – British Library
16th November 2015

∼ঌ An Original English Mawlid ৯∼

৵ PREFACE ৵
On the History of Mawlid Remembrance

THE PROPHET ﷺ is the centre of Islam; he is not just the deliverer of a message, but the highest manifestation of its teachings, a guide to its application, and – above all – a light that shows the path and saves from the dungeons of darkness. To receive this light, hearts have to be attached to him with love, reverence and knowledge.

This is how the Companions lived their life around him; this is how they became the great individuals that they were. To them, he was everything: a father, a guide, a friend, a protector, a leader and a consultant. He was indeed the inspiration, the support and the hope for all those who knew him. They saw him in the smiles on the faces of the tired, the gentle touch on the heads of the young, as a caring father for the orphans and a protection to everyone from physical and spiritual malaise. No wonder, then, that they were keen to accompany him, listen to every word he uttered, register every action, gesture and smile. They did not transcribe this in books – as many of them did not write – but rather engraved it in their hearts and memories.

The Qur'an encouraged this attachment and highlighted the way to make this love productive; turning it into action plans for reforming the self and purifying the heart by following the best of examples: none other than the Prophet ﷺ himself. To make this possible, the life details of the Prophet ﷺ were known to all. The Companions knew the minutiae of his food habits, his taste in clothing, his sleep patterns, his belongings and even his wives' conversations with him. They recorded with accuracy everything he did or owned – from the description of his bed, blanket and cup, to the description of his teeth, nose and the amount of grey hairs in his head and beard.

They also described how he dealt with friends and enemies, rough and easy individuals, and how he handled the most difficult moments of his life, including loss of his wife and children. All of this was an exposition of their love for him and an attempt to enable future generations to have the same level of following of God's Beloved ﷺ. They saw in him perfection in the full sense of the word, and they celebrated this in poetry, prose and close imitation of his blessed character.

All these events would have been impossible to record had he not been born. Therefore, the scholars of Islam have concluded that the single most important event that happened in history is the birth of the Prophet ﷺ. The majority of scholars are of the opinion that the night of his blessed birth is better than any other night, including the blessed night of power (*laylat al-qadr*), since the latter would not have manifested had the former not occured. They further contend that the night of his birth witnessed his honourable appearance and arrival, while *laylat al-qadr* witnessed the descending of angels; undoubtedly, he ﷺ is the best of all creation including angels themselves.

Celebrating and commemorating his blessed birth in words and deeds was not, therefore, alien to the Muslim community from its earliest days. He himself displayed gratitude for his own blessed birth by fasting the day in which he was born and commenting, *'that is a day in which I was born'.*[1] Speaking of the value of the blessed birth of the Prophet ﷺ, his very own uncle Al-'Abbās recited a few lines in the Prophet's presence, declaring:

> *'And the day you were born, the earth was lit,*
> *Horizons, in radiance, witnessed your glory*
> *Travelling paths of your light and guidance,*
> *We will tell this blessed birth story*[2]

Following the path of their predecessors, generations of the scholars of Islam recorded the events that surrounded the blessed birth, to

---
1 Sahih Muslim
2 Mustadrak al-Hakim

An Original English Mawlid

link the community to their Messenger ﷺ whose birth was a mercy to mankind. These written accounts of his birth story came to be known as *mawalid* – the plural of *mawlid*, which literally means 'birth'.

The first to pen a full *mawlid* masterpiece in the history of Islam was the famous historian and scholar Muhammad b. 'Umar al-Wāqidi (d207H), as noted by Imam al-Suhayli in *Ar-Rawd Al-Unuf*, a book on the biography and life events of the Prophet ﷺ. This was followed by another *mawlid* text by the great Ḥāfiz and scholar Abu Bakr b. Abi 'Āṣim al-Shaybāni (d287H). The authors of these two works lived in the early days of Islam: a proof that writing such works is a tradition of the scholars of orthodox Islam from the time of the Salaf.

This parade of love continued with scholars from all backgrounds writing their accounts of the Prophetic birth story, each one reflecting the style and the accuracy of its author. While the essential events were undisputed, some works included little inaccuracies, due to the standards employed by the writers or their lack of specialisation in transmission critique. Such works were not subjected to the tough procedures of ḥadīth criticism applied by ḥadīth masters and specialists for works on law, *sunan* and theology.

This was not the case, however, when a *mawlid* was written by a specialist or a scholar of higher calibre. These scholars wrote their own accounts of the blessed birth with great accuracy and precision; therefore their works attained wide renown and were received with massive acclaim.

The famous Shafi'ī scholar and Qur'anic sciences master, Al-Ḥāfiz Muhammad b. Al-Jazari (d833H), is one of those whose *mawlid* account is highly regarded and respected. He wrote a medium-length mawlid called *al-Ta'rīf bi al-Mawlid al-Sharīf* and then summarised it in a smaller volume. Another famous scholar is the well-known ḥadīth master Al-Ḥāfiz Zayn Al-Dīn 'Abdur-Rahīm Al-'Irāqi, whose *mawlid* is extremely accurate, as he narrates the events along with the chains of transmission that link him back to the sources and leave no space for disputation.

Scholars of Islam who wrote *mawalid* are indeed innumerable. The famous twentieth century scholar of Morocco, al-Sayyid 'Abdul-Ḥayy Al-Kittāni (d1382H) – who is regarded to be one the great luminaries and specialists in the sciences of ḥadīth transmission – wrote an independent work trying to ennumerate all such works that he managed to locate. In this small bibliographical work, entitled *al-Taʾālif al-Mawlidiyyah* (Writings on the Blessed Birth), he counted and introduced 125 *mawalid*. He concluded, though, that such a number is far below the real amount of *mawalid* that were written throughout the history of Islam. He goes as far as noting that the members of his own family alone wrote more than a hundred works around the Prophet ﷺ and the various aspects of his life and character.

This said, the works that describe his blessed birth – whether poetry and prose – are all in Arabic, Turkish, Persian or other eastern languages. Since Muslims now represent a considerable proportion of the English-speaking world, there is a dire need to have a *mawlid* that is inspired by and written for English readers.

Hence the importance of this *mawlid* – rendered in beautiful poetic language and framed with a unique narrative: *The Soliloquy of the Full Moon*. The symbolism of the moon describing the Prophet's birth – the physical moon relating the story of the metaphorical full moon ﷺ – is a fascinating and beautiful one. The atmosphere is thus one of beauty and elegance; the flow of the narrative unfolds the majestic incidents that occured as the universe welcomed the paragon of beauty and perfection.

The writer of this English mawlid is a gifted young lady whose pen of love will hopefully inspire many people to celebrate the birth of the best of creation in writing and recitation. We, the ungifted ones, can but pray for those who, with their beautiful words, touch our souls and connect us with the Prophet of Peace ﷺ. May Allah grant success to all those who inspire others to do good.

SHAYKH AHMAD SAʿAD AL-AZHARI AL-HASANI
Founder and Director – Ihsan Institute and al-Husna Initiative
OCTOBER 2015

An Original English Mawlid

NAVIGATING POETRY
A Guide to Recital of the Soliloquy

IT IS MY distinct pleasure to introduce this work: the first ever traditional *mawlid* composed in the English language. It was written in Rabi' al-Awwal 1436 – each chapter being composed and performed on the same day during the Winterspring Mawlids: a series of twelve consecutive nights of *mawlid* inspired by Hazrat Ghulam Muhyi al-Din Kazi of South Africa.

Following a discussion about the regretable absence of a *mawlid* celebrating the Prophet ﷺ in English, the young author – only 15 at the time – was inspired to compose it. Modelled after the manner of many classical *mawalid,* it is meant for recitation rather than simple reading, and hence follows the rhythmic structure of long-form panegyric poetry. More specifically, it is an *Alfiyya Mawlidiyya*: a thousand-line poem on early Prophetic biography.

Poetry is the highest human means of expression in any language: a fitting tool, therefore, to describe and celebrate the Beauty of Creation ﷺ.³ There is a wealth of poetic works praising him in Eastern and African languages; yet English poetry has long been bereft in this regard. The Soliloquy of the Full Moon is thus intended to combine the Islamic tradition of *mawlid* with the English tradition of epic poetry – that is: the forms, modes, styles and cadences native to the language of Shakespeare and Milton.

---

3 The Arabic Quran, of course, is Divine speech, not the work of humans!

On Poetic Metre

Given that the art of poetic recitation has been largely forgotten in modern times, there follows a brief introduction to assist reciters, that their enjoyment of the *mawlid's* 'taste' might be maximised. What distinguishes formal (classical) poetry from prose writing is not, as some believe, rhyming of the end words, but rather rhythm. This manifests in two aspects: the first being *stress*: where the accent is placed in each part of a line (known as a 'foot'). The following accents are used in the Soliloquy:

» *Iambic:* stress on the 2ⁿᵈ syllable (*da Dum / da Dum*)
» *Trochaic:* stress on the 1ˢᵗ syllable (*Da dum / Da dum*)
» *Anapaestic:* stress on the 3ʳᵈ syllable (*da da Dum / da da Dum*)
» *Tertius Paeonic:* stress on the 3ʳᵈ of four syllables (*da da Da dum*)

The second aspect – measure (or *metre*) – is how many 'feet' comprise a line; this helps to give a verse its rhythm. The metres used in the *mawlid* are tetrameter, heptameter, and octameter (4, 7 & 8 feet per line respectively). To illustrate the combination of stress and metre, examples are now given from the Soliloquy itself:

» *Trochaic Octameter* (8 feet, 1ˢᵗ syllable stressed):
  HERE is / TA ha / HERE is / YA sin / WRAPPED and / CLOAKED in / NO-ble / veil

» *Anapaestic Heptameter* (7 feet, 3ʳᵈ syllable stressed):
  Twas the ROCKS / and the STONES / each one LIFE- / less yet LOV- / ing the ONE / who on EARTH / would tread LIGHT.

» *Tertius Paeonic Tetrameter* (4 feet, 3ʳᵈ of four syllables stressed):
  I have SOUGHT you / I have WAI-ted / for your NIGHT of / brigh-test GRACE

» *Iambic Heptameter* (7 feet, 2ⁿᵈ syllable stressed):
  Come HEAR- / ken ALL / ye FAITH- / ful HEARTS / to THIS / be-WILD- / dered ONE

Iambic metre is by far the most commonly used in the Soliloquy, and indeed in all of classical English poetry. The *mawlid* switches from

An Original English Mawlid

heptameter to octameter at various points, usually to indicate a particularly dramatic or poignant section. Reciters will certainly notice the difference that an additional foot makes to their recitation!

On Recital

Mawlid is not a spectator sport: at their best, they are participative and immersive, bonding both reciters and audience in shared joy, song and celebration. After recitation of Quran and salawat, therefore, the Soliloquy commences with a sung exhortation to *'come quench your thirsty, weary hearts with the name of the Beloved'*.

The fact that the Soliloquy is entirely in traditionally metred poetry means that, if desired, the *mawlid* can be sung either in part or in its entirety; reciters are free to compose their own. It is highly recommended, however, that all participants are encouraged to sing along with the Soliloquy refrain (*'O Lord Most High do sanctify...'*) and the songs (*qasa'id*) that intersperse the chapters, such as *'the Lordly Lineage,' 'the Ascension,'* and so forth. Some of these may be found online.

The Refrain is sung at the ending of each chapter and is not to be confused with the refrains of individual songs, which are placed at their head and should be sung after each verse.

The Benediction (*'Salli ya rabbi wa sallim 'ala nabiyyina...'*) may be sung at any point in the *mawlid* – perhaps especially when reciters need to catch their breath! While the *mawlid* is designed to be participative, it is important that the Quranic verses are read aloud by a single reciter, whilst others listen intently, as per the Quranic injunction.

Throughout the poem and especially in the early chapters, one will find that some of the beautiful names of the Prophet ﷺ – as recorded in the *Dala'il al-Khayrat*, may Allah bless its compiler – have been woven into the text. These are distinguished from the rest of the poem and their Arabic form is written in the margin beside them. Changes in poetic metre and rhythm are similarly signified in the margins with traditional symbols. Footnotes have also been used to explain archaic or difficult words, as well as for points potentially requiring further explanation – as identified by those scholars who have verified the Soliloquy, especially Shaykh Ahmad Sa'ad al-Azhari.

It is the tradition of the righteous during *mawlid* celebrations that participants stand out of respect for the Prophet ﷺ during the description of his blessed birth itself. This place of standing is signalled both in the words of the poem and in the directions. After the *qasida* 'the Blessed Birth' has been sung, it is recommended that further *salawat* be recited as desired, after which all gathered may take their seats again.

The Soliloquy has also been structured flexibly, so that it can be performed in any setting – from family gatherings to large formal events – either at one sitting or in parts over a few days. The original method of recitation was in the first twelve days of Rabi' al-Awwal; to facilitate this, the poem is arranged into a Prologue and twelve chapters, ending with a closing supplication. A complete recitation in one sitting should take about 90 minutes.

Nonetheless, there is no particular requirement that the entire *mawlid* be read at one sitting – participants may choose to recite any of the chapters as a stand-alone segment. As per Islamic etiquette, the *mawlid* should commence and end with the name of Allah, His praise and benedictions upon His Messenger ﷺ.

May Allah take into His endless grace and sublime presence all those who taught, transmitted and embodied the nature and truth of His Emissary ﷺ, all the orators, poets and prosaists who were inspired by love and inspired in turn the love of others for the Beloved ﷺ; and all those who listened to their words and imbibed their meanings.

Lastly, I pray that you will find joy, solace and spiritual refreshment in this remembrance of the life of the Best of all Creation ﷺ, and ask you not to forget the author, her family, teachers and all believers in your duas. The Prophet ﷺ said, *'when the righteous are remembered, mercy descends'* – may we be counted among those who remember and those who receive!

Asim Yusuf (Abu Noor)
Director and Founder – Path to Salvation & Nur al-Habib Foundation
November 2015

An Original English Mawlid

━❦ AUTHOR'S INTRODUCTION ❦━
On the Moon: Sahaba, Mirror and Symbol

'We sent not a Messenger save with the tongue of his people, that he might make clear for them ... so remind them of the Days of God...' [4]

IN THE NAME OF GOD, All-Beneficent, All-Compassionate. All praise and gratitude is due to He who granted me the divine grace to follow, in some small way, those authors who – since olden times – have penned works of love and devotion. Endless peace and blessings on the subject of those works: our Master Muhammad ﷺ, whose birth was unquestionably the greatest bounty that creation has ever received, and on his purified Family, Companions and followers, who exalted his remembrance and carried his message, by word and state, to every corner of the earth.

The Days of God – when Divine Messengers walked the earth and conversed with angels, bearing incomparable wisdom from beyond the heavens, manifesting miracles at their hands – found their pinnacle in the earthly life of the Final Messenger ﷺ, whose very life was miraculous. Though those days are past, there are traces that remain on this earth: the light and wisdom held within the hearts of the people of God. Yet who remains, accessible to all, who holds within their soul the earthly *vision* of the Best of Creation? None, save one.

When a song of praise and love for the Prophet ﷺ is sung, it is not long before one hears mention of the moon. Which poet will leave the

---
4 Ibrahim 14:4-5

moon aside and forsake its story, neglect the night it was chosen and blessed by the Prophet ﷺ? When the men were gathered in the desert, they called to the Prophet ﷺ, '*show us a sign!*' The Messenger of Allah turned his gaze to the moon, hanging argent in the sky. At his gesture, it split apart, each half falling on either side of the mountain, then rose back up again and was formed anew.

Since that time, the moon has become inextricably linked with the Prophet of Allah ﷺ. There is a secret in *suhba*: the companionship of the Prophet ﷺ. To be a companion is not to have seen him, but to have *been* seen by him. What abided in the gaze of the Prophet ﷺ, so transformative in its nature that a mere glance could cause hearts to be filled with certainty and adoration? What secret of love was transferred in that blessed glance? We benighted ones cannot know.

But we do know that the moon was seen by the Prophet ﷺ and gave its sincere shahada – by dying unto itself and then living again as Allah desired. This same moon traversing the heavens is seen by all upon the earth and is veiled from none. Look at the mercy of our Beloved ﷺ: he has left for us one of his companions! For the moon is a *Sahabi*; the very last that remains that may be seen on any clear night. The sun and stars have no ardent face of unchanging rock, but only flame and gases that unceasingly move and disperse in the wide fields of the galaxies. But the moon remains: a mirror physically reflecting the light of the sun, but spiritually reflecting the *Nur Muhammadi*.

In this way, the moon is not merely a sahaba, but a symbol of the secret of Prophetic inheritance. As it is the nature of the moon to reflect light, it is the nature of hearts – once polished and burnished by a lifetime of remembrance and worship – to reflect the divine light of Prophetic guidance. This reflected radiance is in turn reflected by other clean and polished mirror-hearts; in this way the light will travel in every direction and reach the darkest corners. When you look upon the mirror of the moon – when you hear this tale he has to tell – consider this: as long as there are mirrors, the light of the Prophet ﷺ will endure forever. So let us reflect, that we might reflect!

I know another mirror. A man who spent seventy years cleaning and polishing his heart, until not a speck remained of anything other than this Prophetic radiance. What you have read in these pages is from him; what you will read in the coming pages is also from him. Not one verse was written except that he taught it, heard it, or even wrote it himself. The first line of this *mawlid* – not the first you will read, but the first that was written – is his. We have heard that the *Awliya Allah* write secrets into their verses, and we may find these as we read and recite. Let it be that, in this way, we receive some of what they have received and that, as we read and recite, their concentration fixes on us and we become those to whom the Prophetic light transfers. May we be of those about whom the Prophet ﷺ said,

'They yearn for me and I yearn for them – my beloveds!' 'We are your companions,' said the Sahaba, 'but who are your beloveds?' '*They are those who believe in me but have never met me. They are from this tribe and that tribe, this nation and that nation, but they gather together in love for me and depart in love of me.*'

Noor Yusuf
November 2015 / Safar 1437

AN ORIGINAL ENGLISH MAWLID

THE SOLILOQUY of the FULL MOON

Noor Yusuf

❧ EXORDIUM ❧
In God's name do we begin

بِسْمِ اللهِ الرَّحْمٰنِ الرَّحِيمِ

إِنَّا فَتَحْنَا لَكَ فَتْحًا مُّبِينًا ۞ لِيَغْفِرَ لَكَ اللَّهُ مَا تَقَدَّمَ مِنْ ذَنْبِكَ وَمَا تَأَخَّرَ وَيُتِمَّ نِعْمَتَهُ عَلَيْكَ وَيَهْدِيَكَ صِرَاطًا مُّسْتَقِيمًا ۞ وَيَنْصُرَكَ اللَّهُ نَصْرًا عَزِيزًا

لَقَدْ جَاءَكُمْ رَسُولٌ مِّنْ أَنْفُسِكُمْ عَزِيزٌ عَلَيْهِ مَا عَنِتُّمْ حَرِيصٌ عَلَيْكُمْ بِالْمُؤْمِنِينَ رَءُوفٌ رَحِيمٌ ۞ فَإِنْ تَوَلَّوْا فَقُلْ حَسْبِيَ اللَّهُ لَا إِلَهَ إِلَّا هُوَ عَلَيْهِ تَوَكَّلْتُ وَهُوَ رَبُّ الْعَرْشِ الْعَظِيمِ

إِنَّ اللَّهَ وَمَلَائِكَتَهُ يُصَلُّونَ عَلَى النَّبِيِّ ۞ يَا أَيُّهَا الَّذِينَ آمَنُوا صَلُّوا عَلَيْهِ وَسَلِّمُوا تَسْلِيمًا

صَلِّ يَا رَبِّ وَسَلِّمْ عَلَى نَبِيِّنَا ۞ صَلِّ يَا رَبِّ وَسَلِّمْ عَلَى حَبِيبِنَا

THE SOLILOQUY OF THE FULL MOON

QASIDA
THE DAYS OF GOD

Sho - uld auld ac - quain - tan - ce be for - got and ne - ver thought up - on the fla - mes of love wou - ld be put out an - d faith be lost and gone

Sal - li ya Rab - bi wa sal - lim 'a - la na - bi - yi - na! Sal - li ya rab - bi wa sal - lim 'a - la ha - bi - bi - na

An Original English Mawlid

Should auld acquaintance be forgot,
And never thought upon;
The flames of love will be put out,
And faith be lost and gone!

Has thy sweet heart now grown so cold,
That loving breast of thine?
That silent falls thy tongue in praise
Of the Mercy to mankind

صَلِّ يَا رَبِّ وَ سَلِّمْ عَلَى نَبِيِّنَا
صَلِّ يَا رَبِّ وَ سَلِّمْ عَلَى حَبِيبِنَا

Our love for him does no begin
Our love it does no end
We'll sing of our love for him
Till the end of every end

صَلِّ يَا رَبِّ وَ سَلِّمْ عَلَى نَبِيِّنَا
صَلِّ يَا رَبِّ وَ سَلِّمْ عَلَى حَبِيبِنَا

On our beloved Messenger
The Mercy to the Worlds
We'll raise our voices joyfully
In praise and thankfulness

Come join with us, my trusty friends
Come drink from our cups
Come quench your thirsty, weary hearts
With the name of the Beloved

صَلُّوا عَلَى مُحَمَّدٍ صَلُّوا يَا أَحِبَّاء
صَلُّوا عَلَى مُحَمَّدٍ تَنَالُوا رَحْمَة

THE SOLILOQUY OF THE FULL MOON

God's peace on you, O Prophet mine
God's love, O Muhammad
And blessings till the end of time
And my love to you, Ahmad!

صَلُّوْا عَلَى مُحَمَّدٍ صَلُّوْا يَا أَحِبَّآء
صَلُّوْا عَلَى مُحَمَّدٍ تَنَالُوْا رَحْمَةً

Give me your hand, my trusty friend
And here's a hand o' mine
Let's sing a song of love for him
For the mercy to mankind

صَلِّ يَا رَبِّ وَ سَلِّمْ عَلَى نَبِيِّنَا
صَلِّ يَا رَبِّ وَ سَلِّمْ عَلَى حَبِيْبِنَا

For auld lang syne my friends –
Those days of God gone by –
For friends of God and blessed souls
God praise and glorify! [5]

---

5 It felt appropriate to commence this mawlid with a traditional tune. The great Scottish poet, Robert Burns (1759-1796), said, *'this song – an old song of the olden times, which has never been in print – until I took it down from an old man...'*
Auld lang syne means 'for the sake of days long past', which is as apt a description as any for a poem whose purpose is to remind of and celebrate the times of the Blessed Prophet ﷺ and his companions – the 'Days of God' that we are told to remind about.
Some of the native lyrics and dialectical forms have been retained (like *'a hand o' mine'*, *'does no begin'*) to preserve the feel of the original, and the rest have been composed to serve as an *exhortatio* – sung at the commencement of the mawlid to open the hearts of listeners and encourage participation in the beautiful tale that is to come.

An Original English Mawlid

THE REFRAIN

بسم الله الرحمن الرحيم

─❦ PROLOGUE ❦─

In which I narrate all of the conversation that, one night, I partook in with the full moon, in which he[6] described the most perfect of Prophets 🕌

Iambic Heptameter

COME HEARKEN, all ye faithful hearts, to this bewildered one!
And to this tale of ancient days, do listen and pay heed:
The silvern moon in radiant fullness I did call upon,
As, sailing through the sea of heaven, rose he in the east.

O silvern Moon, do cast your gaze upon this seeking one,
Deprived of all my wits – alas! – bereft of certainty.
There is a restless yearning that has settled in my heart
Disturbing all tranquility and haunting every dream
Yet as for that I wish to know, I am unknowing still;
So hear me - I implore, O Moon - and answer with goodwill.'

'I hear your cry,' the Moon replied, 'your earnest bid is heard.
Your boldness and your brave request have stirred me unto words
I ask you now of your distress, your disarray of thought:
What is this great disquiet that has led you to my door?'

'There is a name upon my tongue: I've heard it in the trees,
A murmur passing in the boughs and passing on the leaves.

---
6   Though considered feminine in English, the moon is grammatically masculine in Arabic.

❧ THE SOLILOQUY OF THE FULL MOON ❧

I've heard it on the gentle waves that softly kiss the strand,
And on each blade of swaying grass, a-dance within the wind.
It's whispered in the golden fields and by the riverside;
And fills the song of nightingales at morn and eventide.

This name – proclaimed – is echoing in caverns, cold and deep,
And borne upon the mighty waves of seven mighty seas.
It's carried by the tempest wild unto the ends of earth,
And roared by forge and furnace in the sun's tremendous blaze.

Some say he was but mortal man – a warrior of old –
Who tribes united with a book and conquered every foe.
Some say he was a Prophet true, one revelation sent;
Yet but for this, in form and state, like unto other men.[7]

Iambic Octameter

But yet another tale is sung
    By voices reverent, quavering;
By men weighed down with beards like snow,
    Their eyes alight with wisdom's glow;
In voices frail recalling clear
    A memory passed through hearts of men,
And passed down in a mother's milk
    To infants nursing at the breast.
The secret of a love divine,
    A love profound, a love sublime:

Primordial light adoring God
    Before the Pen in timeless halls,[8]

---

[7] This quatrain describes some of the erroneous views held by people about the Prophet ﷺ, confused as to whether he was a simple historical figure or mere deliverer of a Message; the next passage celebrates the reverential perspective of traditional Islam.

[8] A reference to the narration: *'O Jabir! The first thing God created was my light,'* (Musannaf Abd al-Razzaq) and similar narrations. Individually, these are differed upon, but their collective meaning – the primordial luminous nature of the Prophet ﷺ – has found widespread acceptance among traditionists. It is not considered a doctrinal issue, but rather one of *manaqib* – honouring of the Prophet ﷺ.

An Original English Mawlid

Till into Adam's loins was cast,
    Through seeds of lordly Prophets passed,[9]
At last emerged from faithful womb,
    To shine beyond Arabian dawn:

The Seal of Messengers Divine,
    Harbinger of the end of times!
The first to rise and to prostrate
    Before the Throne for all men's sake
And first to speak and intercede
    Before the Lord as He decreed.[10]

I have sought you; I have waited
    For your night of brightest grace –
Not in waning, nor in waxing;
    Neither crescent young or old,
But a night when you are radiant
    And splendorous in fullness –
That you might relate your memories
    Of him you did behold.

Tertius
Paeonic
Tetrameter

O Lord Most High, do sanctify the one Prophetic Seal,
And, with your grace, perfume the place his blessed form conceals.
And elevate and consecrate and hallow ever more
Madinah's earth, Jerusalem, and blessed Umm al-Qura,
Exalting he whose sandal made them pure.

---

9 Musnad Abi 'Amr and others. For further discussion, see Khafaji and Qari's respective commentaries on the Shifa of 'Iyad (1:428-435)
10 Bukhari the Hadith of the Great Intercession

~ THE BEAUTIFUL NAMES ~

In which the full moon speaks of his deep yearning for the most perfect of Prophets and extolls his virtues by mention of some of his beautiful names.

Iambic Heptameter

BEFORE I did learn how to shine, I'd weep in shroud of night;
I did not care to dazzle – nay! – I would have gone on, fain.[11]
I'd not have mourned my scarcity of clear celestial light,
Except I feared that Ahmad would not gaze on one so plain.

Oh! How shall I describe this man, most perfect of all men?
How shall I praise him who is praised again and time again?[12]
His name, so long, has been engraved upon mine own rock face,
My light is but what I reflect from his emblazoned grace

I have not spoken of this soul – may peace upon him rest! –
Not since he, once, upon me gazed: my dawn had come, my death.[13]
But now the knot of silence has been loosened from my tongue;
O Hamid! Ahmad! Praiser, Praised: your praises shall be sung!

If stars were true in orbit, then they would have circled him –
For from him radiated light – unceasing, never dim.

---

11 *fain*: willing – the unusual positioning is to fulfil the demands of rhyme structure
12 A subtle indication to the meaning of the name Muhammad – meaning 'praised incessantly and continuously – which no Arab before his time was given.
13 A poetic reference to the splitting of the moon at his hand, as described in scripture

THE SOLILOQUY OF THE FULL MOON

Were men to be revered, as were the kings of high renown
Has ever lived, than he, one more deserving of this crown?

How I did weep when it was said to him, 'you are the moon.'
'Except the moon is scarred!' I cried to him, in deepest pain.
'You are the brightest lamp, unblemished; though I shine at night
Your light is such that night itself must flee and turn to day!'

I heard his name - it was the second name I ever heard;
I heard it and it struck my core; the rock upon me cracked,
And dust was scattered, sifted, spread throughout my front and back.
And yet remains! The earthquake of his unborn gaze transferred.

For ages long, until his advent came, I quietly stood
Well-stationed, silent, contemplating, waiting, counting time.
The sun would rise, I'd greet her, and I'd greet her as she set
The stars would turn, the clouds would pass; I went on waiting yet
The oceans rose, the mountains fell, and one day man arrived;
And man went on, he lived and died, his children lived and died.
And still I waited, lamp of night, this being my single thought;
His name my single litany - his face I singly sought.

وحيد   I'd heard he was unique of all: Wahid, of perfect trait!
Of perfect character, of quality, unequalled state.
I thought of him, and sought by him, and called the Greatest One
and said, 'Attend! Allah, Allah! Preserve me till he comes!'

Then finally! Then finally! His birth, his dawn arrived!
He, marvellous one! He, perfect being! He, friend of God Sublime
I plummeted from heaven, from my station, and I cried,
ظاهر   Rejoiced and wept and looked on Tahir – purest – and I sighed.
Until he raised his gentle head, his eye met mine - I shied!
I fled away, ashamed beside his splendour, I did hide.

An Original English Mawlid

Ta Ha! Ya Sin! Beloved friend!
    My love for thee shall reach no end.
From first until your final light,
    I never once could kindle night.
How could I, when bestrode the earth
    The prince whose smile all darkness girthed?
How could I when resplendence fine
    Itself had entered to refine?
And to excite each restless soul
    With truth, to guide and to console;
And to dispel the foulest ways,
    To comfort in the darkest days;
And vanquish every dreadful plight,
    Unveil the One Unending Light.

Iambic Octameter

He is **Ta Ha**, he is **Ya Sin**:
    His names are secret, hidden dreams,
Concealed by One most elevated –
    August, lofty, uncreated,
Yet bestowed with grace unfailing
    To all men derailing, ailing –
        Verily he is **Prevailing**!

Here is **Ya Sin**, here is **Ta Ha**:
    Wrapped and cloaked in noble veil.¹⁴
Here is **Tahir**, purest man,
    With purity does he avail.
Here is **'Aqib**, seal of Prophets
    Sent to guide unto the Way;
Here is **Hashir**, to whose feet
    All men will flee on Judgement Day;

Trochaic Octameter

---

14 The 'noble veil' is a reference to the mystery of the abbreviated letters (*al-muqata'at*) that commence many Quranic chapters. Their meanings are unknown, but many commentators aver that Ta Ha means '*Ya Tahir! Ya Hadi!*' and Ya Sin is '*Ya Sayyid*'—Allah knows best.

THE SOLILOQUY OF THE FULL MOON

Here is Mahin,[15] through whose light
    The gloom of *kufr* is effaced.
Here is Wahid, singular,[16]
    And Ahid, written, long presaged.[17]
Here is Hamid, Ahmad, Mahmud:[18]
    Praiser and the one most praised.
Here is one whose name – Muhammad –
    Lofty on the Throne is raised!

Iambic Heptameter

Now hark and listen, traveller, as I shall now narrate
From dawn primæval, verities of him I did await.

O Lord Most High, do sanctify the one Prophetic Seal,
And with your grace, perfume the place his blessed form conceals.
And elevate and consecrate and hallow ever more
Madinah's earth, Jerusalem, and blessed Umm al-Qura,
Exalting he whose sandal made them pure.

---

15 *Mahin*, *Hashir* and *Aqib*, along with their meanings, are narrated in Bukhari and Muslim, as well as the names Ahmad and Muhammad, by the Prophet ﷺ himself.
16 *Wahid*: unique in nature and attribute
17 *Ahid*: a name of the foretold Prophet found in previous scriptures
18 All these names are derived from *hamd*, meaning praise. *Ahmad*, in particular, may entail: one whose nature is praiseworthy, is always praising, or is most praiseworthy.

An Original English Mawlid

الفَصْلُ الثَّانِي

─◦ THE PRAYER OF IBRAHIM ◦─

In which is described the building of the Ka'bah by Ibrahim and Isma'il, and their fervent prayer for a Prophet to be sent to their descendants.

Iambic Heptameter

I ASK YOU of your knowledge—has it reached your straining ears:
How prayers were called from Bakkah's[19] vale and borne on desert winds,
Aloft until they reached the higher platforms of the skies,
Where seraphim,[20] celestial attendants, beat their wings,

Ascending higher, spreading word – the word of Ibrahim,
Who stood upon a hovering stone with dust upon his hands,
And dust upon his blessed robe, and water on his brow -
And too the word of Isma'il, beside his father, blessed
Alike with mantling of prophethood, divine address?

The angels, ornamented, feather-wingèd did confer
Amongst themselves upon the Prophets' earnest orison.[21]
Indeed, a seraph of their midst had once embarked to earth,
Conveying news upon his tongue, and rock upon his back:
This starless weight of ebon from Abu Qubays's hill
Had long declined from Eden, alabaster-bright, until

---

19 Bakkah was the original name of Makkah, and it is referred to as such in the Quran
20 *seraphim*: angels, the singular being *seraph*
21 *orison*: supplication or prayer

THE SOLILOQUY OF THE FULL MOON

The darkly deeds of Adam's scions[22] rapidly immersed
The sacred mass and blackened it - withal, it was preserved
And carried by the angel to the hand of Ibrahim
Who placed it in his mighty house - the Ka'bah - he had raised;[23]

He, Prophet and his Prophet son – those highest-stationed men! –
This hallowed host of heaven did reflect upon their words:
Did they know of the Greater Will? Did they know of the plan
Inscribed, incised and destined on the Tablet by the Pen?
The predetermination of the answer to their call.
Yea, when the angels heard of it, they'd wept with awe, enthralled!

Iambic Octameter

By virtue of his dear Friend,
    Allah Exalted would attend
And answer the sincere plea
    By course most manifest, supreme;
For God Almighty had decreed
    That He'd to Bakkah's vale bequeath
The most superlative bequest!
    Such was the Prophets' true request:

'O Lord Most High, accept from us;
    Thou art the Hearing, Knowing One!
May we and our progeny
    Submit ourselves unto Thy way,
Reveal to us exalted sacraments
    That we may Thee obey;
Accept from us our penitence,
    For art not Thou Beneficent?
For nations of our offspring, send
    A Prophet from amongst themselves

---

22 *scion*: a descendant
23 The passage as a whole details the descent of the Black Stone (*al-hajr al-aswad*) from Paradise to Abu Qubays, a mountain in Makka, where it was placed in the Ka'ba by Ibrahim and Isma'il. Initially pure white, it was blackened by the sins of humanity.

An Original English Mawlid

Who shall recite Thy verses high,
    And teach Thy Book, and sanctify,
Transmitting wisdom; verily,
    Thou art Almighty, Wise!'

| Recite al-Baqara: 127–129 |

وَإِذْ يَرْفَعُ إِبْرَاهِيمُ ٱلْقَوَاعِدَ مِنَ ٱلْبَيْتِ وَإِسْمَٰعِيلُ رَبَّنَا تَقَبَّلْ مِنَّآ إِنَّكَ أَنتَ ٱلسَّمِيعُ ٱلْعَلِيمُ ۞ رَبَّنَا وَٱجْعَلْنَا مُسْلِمَيْنِ لَكَ وَمِن ذُرِّيَّتِنَآ أُمَّةً مُّسْلِمَةً لَّكَ وَأَرِنَا مَنَاسِكَنَا وَتُبْ عَلَيْنَآ إِنَّكَ أَنتَ ٱلتَّوَّابُ ٱلرَّحِيمُ ۞ رَبَّنَا وَٱبْعَثْ فِيهِمْ رَسُولًا مِّنْهُمْ يَتْلُوا۟ عَلَيْهِمْ ءَايَٰتِكَ وَيُعَلِّمُهُمُ ٱلْكِتَٰبَ وَٱلْحِكْمَةَ وَيُزَكِّيهِمْ إِنَّكَ أَنتَ ٱلْعَزِيزُ ٱلْحَكِيمُ

O Lord Most High, do sanctify the one Prophetic Seal,
And with your grace, perfume the place his blessed form conceals.
And elevate and consecrate and hallow ever more
Madinah's earth, Jerusalem, and blessed Umm al-Qura,
Exalting he whose sandal made them pure.

THE SOLILOQUY OF THE FULL MOON

⁓ QASIDA ⁓
THE LORDLY LINEAGE

An Original English Mawlid

| Refrain |

Salla Allāhu ʿala Muhammad
Sallallāhu ʿala Tāha Khayri al-khalqi kulli himi
Sallallāhu ʿala Tāha wa ālihi wa sahbihi

God's blessings be on *Muhammad*, the Prophet who was born
Of Aminah and *Abdullah*, who never saw his son.
And he of *Abdul Muttalib*, whose true name was Shayba,
And he the son of *Hashim*, he the son of *Abd Manaf*.

| Refrain |

Son of *Qusayy*, son of *Kilab* - but Hakim was his name -
He *Murra's* son, the son of *Ka'b*, the scion of *Lu'ayy*
The son of *Ghalib*, son of *Fihr* - from whose given name
The people dwelt in Makkah's vale were named as the Quraysh.

| Refrain |

He son of *Malik*, son of *Nadr*, son of *Kinana*
And he the son of *Khuzayma*, the son of *Mudrika*,
Of *Ilyas* born, he *Mudar's* son, who of *Nizar* was born,
The son of *Ma'ad*, who of *Adnan's* progeny was come.

| Refrain |

Beyond Adnan we do not go in naming the ascent
Of Muhammad – upon him peace – but many fathers thence
From his own speech, the Truthful One narrated that he was
The answered prayer of Isma'il and of the Friend of God.

| Refrain |

O Muslims, learn! This was the way of generations past
To know the Prophet's forefathers right up unto Adnan.
May He who sent the Prophet with the truth accept from us
This litany of those who bore the light of Muhammad.[24]

| Refrain |

---

24 This is indeed a Sunnah of the Prophet ﷺ and generations of the righteous who followed him. He said, *'I have emerged from pure loins and pure wombs – naught of the taint of Jahiliyya has touched me.'* He also named his lineage up to Adnan, before saying, *'after this, the genealogists lie,'* though the descent of the Arabs from Ibrahim and Isma'il is well known.

An Original English Mawlid

الفَصْلُ الثَّالِثُ

‿ THE PROPHET'S LINEAGE ‿

In which is discussed the nobility of the Prophet's ﷺ genealogy, the virtues of his immediate ascendants, and the dream of Abdul Muttalib that led to the rediscovery of the well of Zamzam.

Iambic Heptameter

OFTENTIMES I'd ponder this outstanding line of men,
How each did bear within his soul this one transcendent light.
A lineage untarnished; men and women of their times
Were chosen by their purity for this offspring sublime.

The Makkan kingship, Arab crown, was not but twice proffered:
The first time to Qusayy - 'The Wise' - distinguished of his day;
The pride of both his fathers, lordly chieftain of the Vale.
Thereafter reigned no king until a throne again was bid
When leaders bade the Messenger refrain from his Message.

'Were sun and moon placed in my hands, I still would not surcease.'
(They should have known: I *was* within his hand, beneath his feet!)
He needed not their diadem – for him was all renown!
Since unremembered time he was Be-turbaned with the Crown!

صَاحِبُ التَاجِ

See Hashim, this magnific man! The Arabs called for him
To lead them, for they saw he bore a light that did not dim.
And when he married Salma, greatest woman of her age,
Madinah did wed Makkah, and two blessed bonds were made.

THE SOLILOQUY OF THE FULL MOON

And Abdul Muttalib was named as Shayba from his youth.²⁵
A grey-haired child of wisdom far surpassing all with truth!
Know you of how an inspiration reached him in a dream?
He lay at rest, this lofty man, beside the Hallowed House.
Right there, before his eyes, a figure came to him and spoke,

'Dig purity!' but said no more; it vanished. He awoke
With peace within his heart and so resolved to stay again.
Again, it came: 'Dig righteousness!' 'But what is this?' he said.
A third time: 'Dig the treasured hoard!' then, finally, a fourth:
'Dig Zamzam!' said the spectre. 'What is Zamzam?' called he forth.²⁶

Iambic Octameter

'Dig Zamzam, dig her, righteous, pure;
    Dig Zamzam, dig the treasured hoard.
She has been far too long repressed -
    Your father Isma'il's bequest -
She shall not dry, she does abound
    To ever quench the pilgrim crowd.'
Behold! The wellspring, pristine, rife;
    The earth's effused abundance, life;
The Ka'bah's treasure long concealed –
    Glad Tidings came as it unsealed.

Perceive the secret of the time that Zamzam did cascade;
She'd waited for the promised one, a bride at last unveiled.
Now heed the word of He Most High as he does say, *'Rejoice!
In blessings and the mercy.'* Yea, in this do now reflect:
'It does surpass all that unto themselves they do collect!'

---

25 The grandfather of the Prophet ﷺ was named *Shaybat al-Hamd*, because he was born with naturally gray hair. Hashim's wife Salma had married him only on condition that she could remain in her native town of Yathrib, and it was there that her child was born. Hashim fell victim to the fever of Yathrib, and when his brother Muttalib brought his nephew back to Makka, someone asked him if he had bought a slave. He laughed, but the nickname stuck: his nephew became known as 'the servant of Muttalib.'

26 During one of the ancient conflicts, the treasures of the Ka'bah were thrown into the well, and it had been covered over. Centuries later, Zamzam was little more than myth.

An Original English Mawlid

The blessing was the treasure and the mercy, Zamzam's surge;
But greatest Spring of Bliss, the Mercy was to yet emerge!

The truth was spoken clear by him Of Blessèd Origin
'My Lord has guarded me within the noblest descent
For never has there branched a lineage but I was sent
Into the nobler line until the time I should emerge
Through wedded bond, my parentage, preservèd I have come.'[27]
He surely is the Hoped-for, the Select of the Elect![28]

| Recite Yunus: 58 |

قُلْ بِفَضْلِ ٱللَّهِ وَبِرَحْمَتِهِۦ فَبِذَٰلِكَ فَلْيَفْرَحُوا۟ هُوَ خَيْرٌ مِّمَّا يَجْمَعُونَ

O Lord Most High, do sanctify the one Prophetic Seal,
And with your grace, perfume the place his blessed form conceals.
And elevate and consecrate and hallow ever more
Madinah's earth, Jerusalem, and blessed Umm al-Qura,
Exalting he whose sandal made them pure.

---

27 Narrated *musalsal* through the family of the Prophet ﷺ in the Musnad of 'Adani, as well as by Abu Nu'aym and Tabarani. Other narrations mention similar wordings.
28 As per Wathila's narration from the Prophet ﷺ: 'Verily, Allah selected Kinana from the descendants of Isma'il, and selected Quraysh from the tribe of Kinana, and selected the Banu Hashim from the Quraysh, and selected me from the Banu Hashim.' (Muslim)

الفَصْلُ الرَّابِعُ

~ THE YEAR OF THE ELEPHANT ~

In which is discussed the attempted assault and destruction of the Ka'bah by Abrahah and God's preservation of His House: all this in the year of the blessed Prophet's ﷺ birth.

Iambic Heptameter

SO! KNOW you of the histories abounding Makkah's lands?
Those marvellous, miraculous events that did precede
The greatest of arrivals? Held in living memory
Of those who soon would walk with him and who his call received.

Erstwhile the Abyssinian king held Yemen in his reign.
A leader of a kingdom of the Christians was he.
Now, clearly mark the vicegerent this Negus did proclaim
As ruler of the Yemenis – was Abrahah his name.

He'd heard within the barren wilderness of Makkah's dell,
There towered high the House of God attended by all men
Who walked abroad and unto it with sacrifice and wealth,
As gifts and hence the desert vale did thrive and flourish well.

And Abrahah resentfully did widen jealous eyes,
And wave his hand to San'a in the south where he devised
To thence erect a glorious cathedral to divert
The pilgrims from the House of Ibrahim into his church.

THE SOLILOQUY OF THE FULL MOON

But works of human vanity can never quench the urge
Deep-rooted in the hearts of men to travel forth in search
Of that most blessed valley where their eldest father stood
And called on his Creator for the first time on the earth.[29]

And so confounded, Abrahah, to quench his rival thirst,
Led out his men to desecrate the Ka'bah that he cursed.
So northward marched his army, desolation in their hearts,
And devastation's whetting flame ignited on their blades,

Until, on drawing nigh to Makkah's valley did they halt,
And called upon the chieftain of Quraysh to then walk forth.
So standing tall, his bearing strong, rose Abdul Muttalib
And Abrahah, impressed, descended his high throne to greet
This noble man of noble stance, to whom he'd favour grant
If such was asked – and asked it was by this imposing chief.

'Return to me the hundred camels stolen from my hand,'
Said he, but Abrahah was disenchanted by his words.
'Why do you seek this temporal, irreverent request
When axes overloom your faith?' But Shayba did reply:

'I am lord of this camel flock, the Ka'bah has its Lord,
As I protect what's mine, He shall defend His from your horde.'
Said Abrahah, 'your Lord cannot defend his House from me.'
But Shayba said, 'my camels? Abrahah, we soon shall see!'

The Makkans fled to refuge in the hills beyond the town
But those remaining found their solace at the Ka'bah's ground
With Abdul Muttalib, they grasped the House's metal door,
'We slaves protect our houses: now protect Your house, O Lord!'

---

29 Tradition reports that it was at this very spot that Adam ﷺ was sent down to earth and prayed for the first time. Either in the valley of Bakkah itself, or at Arafat, he sought forgiveness by the name of Muhammad Rasulullah, and his Lord turned to him in mercy, as reported in the tafsir of Qurtubi and others, as well as Ibn al-Jawzi in *al-Wafa*,

An Original English Mawlid

The regent, Abrahah, awaited haughtily the end
Of Makkah's fame and looked upon his elephant in pride.
The mighty beast! Majestic, richly-decked, Mahmud his name
Was, unconstrainèd, grandly turned to ruin and defame.

    Alas for them! When Mahmud saw
        The Ka'bah, eminent, ahead
    He did not march, he would not charge
        Nor strike, but dropped his garnished head.
    The regent's army were outraged
        As Mahmud thwarted their rampage!

    They beat and struck but naught achieved,
        And failed when they sought to deceive;
    The beast held fast against this horde,
        Defying taunts and hooks and swords
    And when they did command him yield,
        Mahmud, before the Ka'bah, *kneeled*!

In truth! This mighty elephant perceived the Holy House
As whence the Holder of the Highest Rank would soon arrive.
What shaft could pierce like the awe for him, the Piercing Star?
Was he not deeply humbled, in prostration falling far?
If further portent was desired, lo: the darkened skies!

    The army held the land's domain
        But God Almighty sent a bane:
    The hosts of heaven, stalwart birds,
        Arose upon them undeterred
    By arrow mere, sword or spear,
        Pelting stones with force severe.

THE SOLILOQUY OF THE FULL MOON

The army fled! And Abrahah did perish as he ran
And all were wasted save who spread the truth to their own lands.
Yea, Abrahah – so proud – was, by his armoured beast, betrayed.
Heed this! *'Did He not cause their plan to fall to disarray?'*

| Recite al–Fil |

بِسْمِ ٱللَّهِ ٱلرَّحْمَٰنِ ٱلرَّحِيمِ

أَلَمْ تَرَ كَيْفَ فَعَلَ رَبُّكَ بِأَصْحَٰبِ ٱلْفِيلِ ۞ أَلَمْ يَجْعَلْ كَيْدَهُمْ فِى تَضْلِيلٍ ۞ وَأَرْسَلَ عَلَيْهِمْ طَيْرًا أَبَابِيلَ ۞ تَرْمِيهِم بِحِجَارَةٍ مِّن سِجِّيلٍ ۞ فَجَعَلَهُمْ كَعَصْفٍ مَّأْكُولٍ

How perfectly Allah Most High preserved the Ka'bah's form!
How soon the nigh Reviver would the Ka'bah's heart transform!
Observe how all did fall except for him who did submit:
Mahmud! And, evermore, 'twas named Year of the Elephant.

Count forty days, for forty passed until the worlds did cry
In joy and gladness as arrived the Gift of God Most High!

O Lord Most High, do sanctify the one Prophetic Seal,
And with your grace, perfume the place his blessed form conceals.
And elevate and consecrate and hallow ever more
Madinah's earth, Jerusalem, and blessed Umm al-Qura,
Exalting he whose sandal made them pure.

An Original English Mawlid

الفَصْلُ الخَامِسُ

～ THE BLESSED BIRTH ～

In which is described the primordial Muhammadan Light, as well as the signs and wonders that accompanied his birth, and in which God's blessings and mercy are reverentially celebrated.

Iambic Heptameter

BUT FIRST, a moment spend in grief, for 'Abdullah had passed.
The son belov'd who from the sacrifice[30] was saved, to pass
From father's loins to mother's womb the long-awaited light
That blazed beyond the stars, dispelling ignorance's night.
He fell to Yathrib's ailment, in a fever, and he died
Not once to see his son, nor once again his widowed bride.

AND now my words do falter and my eager tongue grows quiet,
For how shall I describe the dawn of this primæval Light?

نور

In timeless time ere aught did pass and God, there was but Him,
A soul he made from His own Light[31] – a light that would not dim:
The Promised One, his words like shining pearls of wisdom strewn;
Emissary of the Sovereign Lord; one wreathed with stars and moons.

مُتَأَمَّل

رَسُول

---

30 As a child, 'Abdullah – the most beloved of Abdul Muttalib's ten sons – had been miraculously saved from being sacrificed in fulfillment of a vow, his life spared in exchange for 100 camels. Thus the Prophet ﷺ would say, '*I am the son of the two sacrificial ones*' – these being his own father and his forefather Isma'il ﷺ ('Asqalani deemed the wording strong overall).
31 Doctrinally, this means that God created a light from His uncreated, pre-eternal attribute of *Nur*, not that God's light was somehow 'split'. In similar fashion, the Quran speaks of God '*blowing something of His spirit*' into Adam ﷺ. The phrase signifies a special honour.

 THE SOLILOQUY OF THE FULL MOON

That pure light – it was quartered: thrice and then a time again,
And from it sprung the Tablets, Throne, Divine Court and the Pen;
The Garden blossomed in that spring; the Fire was ignited;
The Skies outspread, the humble Earth no longer was benighted.

 The visages of lovers were illuminated next,
And then the rays shone on their tongues, and deep within their breasts.³²

And finally, in Purest Soul, He placed the Beacon light;
He was the Gilded Crown of men and such the Pen did write.

'When was your Prophethood?' 'Twas asked within his earthly days.
Said he, 'when Adam was between the water and the clay.'³³
'If not for you!' – Be mindful of His elevated words,
'If not for you, I'd not have made the heavens and the earth!'³⁴

Who else may manifest the Lordly mercy, gentle light?
Who else may manifest the Lordly majesty and might?
In truth! His sake the dearest sake! What may I do but sigh?
If not for him there'd be no Badr – full moon shining high!

Iambic Octameter

    There shooting through the deepest night
        Went kindled arrows in defence.
    The lucent stars drew close to earth;
        The men, in awe, watched their descent.
    The heavens were secured by angels
        From the wicked Jinn obscured,
    And I descended so to gaze
        On him for whom I'd long endured.

---

32 A reference to the Covenant of Prophethood, mentioned in the Quran (Aal Imran 3:81), when the souls of all the Prophets were called before God and granted Prophethood on condition that they testify to the Final Messenger ﷺ, as narrated by Ibn Abi Hatim.
33 A narration from the Musnad Ahmad (al-Shamiyyin). The more famous version, from Jami al-Tirmidhi and others, states, '...when Adam was between spirit and body.'
34 The scholars of hadith reject this specific wording but affirm its meaning in many of their works: see 'the Encyclopaedia of Islamic Doctrine' volume 2 for further details.

An Original English Mawlid

Perceive the signs that did surround
        His dawning, beautified and pure:
In Ctesiphon, the citadel,
        The ceilings held aloft derailed,
Thus riving balconies – assailed! –
        As he, the Chosen One, prevailed.
The peaks and vales were filled with light,
        The stars shone undiminished, bright.

The courts of Persia were subdued
        As Magian priests failed to construe
Why, since a thousand years ablaze,
        Extinguished was their sacred flame.
The Lake of Sawa, once so vast
        It hosted ships, did dry to sand,
While Vale Samawa, desolate,
        O'erflowed and water gushed a-strand.
And Caesar's palaces in Shaam
        Were radiant and clear to see
By Amina, resplendent mother,
        As she lay in reverie.

She heard, 'within your womb you hold this people's lord, so say
Upon his birth: 'I place him in the refuge of the One
Against the evil of the envier.' And this his name...'

Iambic Heptameter

What is his name? It surely is the loftiest of names!
Indeed he ever was a Mercy sent unto the world;
While yet unborn he was Concerned for her whom he so loved.
The Lover and Beloved did console her in her grief,
Preserving her from sorrow, granting solace, rest, relief.

That which travails in pregnancy did never once assail.
He is the One Enshrouded, ever then does he enshroud;
He is the One Enwrapped, yea, ever then does he enwrap

THE SOLILOQUY OF THE FULL MOON

In comfort's cloak, his mother – yet unborn he did attend!
She knew him whom she bore: he was Wali, Protecting Friend.

    The time drew nigh and every sky
        Was lit, creation glorifying.

For soon would bloom midst desert bare a single, flowering tree;[35]
The Saviour, Deliverer – mankind he would set free.
Before the dawn his birth approached. To Aminah arrived
The fairest souls to grace the earth, attending at her side.
Came 'Asiya, courageous one, the Pharaoh's pious bride;

And Mary, mother of the Christ, true servant to her Lord;
And all the maids of Paradise she met and she was awed.
Again, before her eyes the mighty lands of Shaam she spied,
And palaces with golden domes that soared up to the sky!

Such marvelling and wonderment she felt in those sweet hours,
And breezes cool, and rapture, and the scent of budding flowers.
Illumination emanated, luminescence radiated;
Joy abounded in the heavens, in the earth and in the seas -

                      And then was silence...
                           Ceasing...
                             Still...

    The spring did rise in Makkah's vale!
        The dawn broke forth, he was unveiled...
    Arise! and Welcome! Do attend!
        And greet the most Beloved Friend!

🌿 Place of Standing 🌿

---

[35] An allusion to the verse, 'Did we not find you *dall*, and guided you?' A beautiful explanation in Qushayri's Tafsir notes that one of the meanings of ضال is *'a solitary flowering tree amidst barren land'* – vegetation, of course, indicating the presence of water, thus life.

An Original English Mawlid

QASIDA
IN THE STILL OF THE NIGHT

In the still of the night did the stars come to earth. And the angels descended to witness the bi-rth
of a light that would shine to the end of all things O believers and lovers send you blessings on him-
Ba la ghal 'u la bi ka ma li - hi du - ja - bi ja - ma li - hi-hi
Ha - su - nat ja - mi - 'u khi sa - li - hi 'a - lay - hi wa aa - li - hi

The tidings were spread to the land and the sea
Believers rejoice! The Revi-

How blessed

THE SOLILOQUY OF THE FULL MOON

| Refrain |

Balaghal ulā bi kamālihi
Kashafa ad-duja bi jamālihi
Hasunat jāmi'u khisālihi
Sallu alayhi wa ālihi

In the still of the night did the stars come to earth,
And the angels descended to witness the birth
Of a light that would shine to the end of all things,
O believers and lovers, send your blessings on him!

The tidings were spread through the lands and the seas;
Creation rejoice! The Reviver is here!
How blessed the dawn! How blessed the morn!
Believers, give thanks, for Muhammad is born!

An Original English Mawlid

| Refrain |

From a winter when faith was not found anywhere,
He would bring such a spring as beyond compare;
And the fruits of his truth would bring peace to the soul.
O believers and lovers, send your blessings on him!

Spread tidings across all the lands and the seas!
O sleepers, awake! The Reviver is here!
How blessed the dawn! How blessed the morn!
Believers, give thanks, that Muhammad was born!

| Refrain |

| Recite Salawāt |

O Lord Most High, do sanctify the one Prophetic Seal,
And with your grace, perfume the place his blessed form conceals.
And elevate and consecrate and hallow ever more
Madinah's earth, Jerusalem, and blessed Umm al-Qura,
Exalting he whose sandal made them pure.

الفَصْلُ السَّادِسُ

~ THE NURSING *of the* PROPHET ~

In which is described the early life and nursing of the blessed Prophet ﷺ by Halimah of Banu Sa'd, as well as the miracle of the splitting of his chest.

Iambic Heptameter

THE ARABS held a custom since the unremembered days
To send their infants to the desert whence they would be raised,
Away from city maladies - pollution - to grow hale
And strong to learn the ancient tongue by Bedouins preserved.

This clean air would the young imbibe and learn the nomad ways,
For nomad men were noble men unsevered from the path
Of liberty; the townsman was imprisoned by the sloth
And heedlessness that lurked and throve within the city walls.
The pure tongue of the Arabs and its eloquence was taught,
By nursemaids of the Banu Sa'd who from the wilds drove forth.

Now! Look upon the desert roads that weary camels track
And see a lonesome camel faltering. Upon her back
A woman and a new-born babe within her tired arms
A crying, hungry child without a single drop to drink
From milkless mother or unyielding camel, gaunt and weak.
The others had outstripped her in the race to Makkah's vale
That through their milk they might form ties of honour with
                                                    Quraysh.

❧ THE SOLILOQUY OF THE FULL MOON ❧

This nurse, Halimah Sa'diyyah, the poorest of her tribe,
Found every Makkan infant fostered when she did arrive.
Nay, all but one. A noble orphan none would take to care;
Unwanted nurse and nursling... if they had been but aware!

Though poverty was undesired, she feared to return
With empty hands, so told her husband Harith, '*I will turn
To Aminah, the widow, though she has but naught to give.*'
Said Harith, '*as you please; perhaps Allah will bless through him.*'

Before Halimah slept a babe enwrapped in purest white
Upon a silken cloth of green and love surged in her heart.
She touched his chest, he woke and smiled, and from him shone a light
That reached the highest heavens; and she raised him to her breast
To drink, though dry, and suddenly her milk did flood within
Abundantly! He drank his fill, she turned him to her left,
But he refused! He knew she had a baby waiting still.
That night, Masruh, Halimah's child, who'd starved for many days
Did drink beside his brother, whom Halimah took to raise.

The bosom of her camel, parched, a-weary, did abound!
And leapt to life, outstripping every other in her charge
Toward the desert. '*Fie, Halimah!*' Banu Sa'ad proclaimed,
'*Some wonder has bechanced her! Is her mount indeed the same?*'
'Twas recognised by Harith and Halimah that, indeed,
The Blessing of Allah had come to them – they would succeed!

There was no earth more barren, nor a land more desolate
Than whence the Bedouins had left, and now did pitch their tents.
But with the advent of the Quenching Rain, the country bloomed;
The pasture-lands did flourish, and Halimah's flocks did graze
On greenest lands, contented, while no other did collect
The increase that the Succour brought, and on this do reflect!

An Original English Mawlid

The mercy of the Prophet, from beginning, was unveiled:
The dead earth sprang to life and restful ease o'ertook travails.³⁶
Though Aminah did miss her son, this wondrous, precious child,
She saw Halimah's love for him and let stay awhile.

HE GREW in perfect kindness, sweetest manners – all did love
This brave and hearty child who spoke the truth and did no wrong.
Then one day came Masruh, Halimah's son, a-flight and scared.
'My brother has been killed! He has been killed!' Masruh declared.
In fear Harith and Halimah ran to find the child,
And there he lay, quite silent, pale and shaking – but alive.

The infant said, *'two men in white did come and down I lay,
They opened up my chest and searched - for what I cannot say.'*
Of tender years was he, but never did they doubt his words
He was the Truthful, Trustworthy, afraid but safe, unhurt.
No sign beside the faintest scar, and 'twixt his shoulderblades:
They saw, upon his back, the Seal of Prophecy engraved.

Two angels had in truth approached him, laid him on the earth
And opened up his breast, then for his blessed heart they searched.
They placed it in a bowl of ice then bathed it with the drops
Of Zamzam's spring, and cast away from it a single spot.

Shaytan was ever banished from the Prophet's purest soul.
The devil never would affect the Messenger or sway,
Nor ever once be interceded for on Judgement Day.³⁷

اَلصَّادِق

اَلْأَمِين

---

36 *travails*: hardship – difficulties were replaced by ease, and the Banu Sa'd had a blessed year of abundance after years of scarcity. Though not mentioned in the mawlid, it is also narrated that whenever the young Prophet ﷺ ate first, there would always be sufficient food for all. These events, like the cloud that shaded him on his travels, are formally known as *irhas* – annunciatory miracles.
37 This is the first splitting of the Prophet's ﷺ chest. The angels – Gibril and Mika'il – removed a black spot from his heart, saying, *'this is Shaytan's portion of him.'* Some scholars

Halimah, terrified, returned to Aminah and spoke
Of these events, but Aminah did laugh her fears away.
She told her nursemaid of the miracles that did occur
Upon the night of spring, the night of his most blessed birth.[38]

ONE DAY, once many years had passed, the Messenger did meet
A woman, old and ailing, eighty years of age who smiled.
He felt a softness in his heart and saw within this smile
So wizened, frail and gentle, one whose heart he recognised.
A heart that had believed, that long had loved him since the sight
Of him, a new-born, in her eighteenth year; had known his light.
'Your features have some change,' he held her hand and sat aside,
'My mother,' said the Prophet and she saw, again, her child.

O Lord Most High, do sanctify the one Prophetic Seal,
And with your grace, perfume the place his blessed form conceals.
And elevate and consecrate and hallow ever more
Madinah's earth, Jerusalem, and blessed Umm al-Qura,
Exalting he whose sandal made them pure.

---

refer this to the removal of the human potentiality for satanic influence, whle others declare that this was the portion of Prophetic intercession for Shaytan on Judgement Day. The splitting of the chest, washing of the heart and the faint scar is narrated by Anas in Muslim.
38 The vision of Aminah, and the other miracles, are reported by 'Irbadh ibn Sariya in Musnad Ahmad, Tabarani and Bayhaqi, and deemed *sahih* by Dhahabi.

An Original English Mawlid

الفَصْلُ السَّابِعُ

—◈ REVELATIONS ◈—

In which is described the seclusion and visions of the Prophet ﷺ just prior to the onset of revelation in the Cave of Hira, as well as its immediate aftermath.

Anapaestic Heptameter

T HE FORTIETH year of the Prophet arrived,
    Every night did he brightly perceive
A dream of distinction as light of the dawn
    That did break; indeed, naught did he see
But that it would occur in his wakefulness,
    Clarion as it would pass in his dreams.
Every vision was true and he witnessed but verities,
    Both in his waking and sleep.
He had sought to retreat to the mountains, secluding
    Himself from all worldly pursuits,
Seeking solace in solitude, worshipping God,
    As his forebears since Isma'il's time.
Many years he had walked on this trail to the mountains
    And silently sat in a cave.[39]

(In first two lines, the stress starts on the 2nd syllable in the 1st foot)

Now this hollow was named as the Cave of Hira –
    He would contemplate there many days.
As he walked in the outskirts of Makkah, he'd hear
    Hidden voices that called unto him,

---

39 This chapter is effectively a transmission of the Hadith of Aisha: Bukhari #3

THE SOLILOQUY OF THE FULL MOON

'Peace upon you, God's Messenger!' such they did cry,
    Yet the criers were always unseen.
'Twas the rocks and the stones! Each one lifeless yet loving
    The one who on earth would tread light;
They would sense him and call him, salute as he passed them
    And long for his most treasured sight.[40]

I DID TURN a new crescent and Ramadhan dawned
    And the Prophet embarked on retreat.
And he sat, in Hira, contemplating Allah;
    He did ponder and praise and entreat.

Then! In glory and majesty, solitude broke
    As one entered the Mountain of Light:
'Twas a visitor, man yet unearthly, ethereal
    Who did command him, *'recite!'*
Our Prophet was deep in reflection on God,
    So he said then, *'I will not recite.'* [41]

But the man came upon him and whelmed[42] him, embraced him
    And squeezed him; again said, *'recite!'*
This embrace was the man's concentration: the Prophet's
    Attention did focus on him,
For he saw then this matter in clarity and he
    Attended, *'I do not recite.'*

---

40 As noted in the Shifa of Qadi 'Iyad, as well as similar in Muslim and Tirmidhi.
41 The well-known position regarding the Prophet's ﷺ repeated statement *'ma ana bi-qari'* is that, each time, it meant *'I do not/cannot recite,'* as mentioned by 'Iyad, Nawawi and others. Abu Shama and others, however, affirm that the *'ma'* in the Prophet's ﷺ statements can be understood as first entailing refusal (*ma nahiya*), then incapability (*ma nahiya*), then questioning (*ma istifhamiyya*), based on variant narrations of the same hadith clearly implying those meanings, as described by Ibn Hajar (*Fath al-Bari* 2:30). This is the position taken in the Solioquy, partially because it makes for better narrative flow, and also because it more clearly implies the effect of the embrace of Gibril, as mentioned by a number of the ulama.
42 *whelm*: overwhelmed him with the power of the embrace – an interpretative translation of *'hatta balaghani al-juhd'* – *'until I reached the limit of my strength.'*

And again did the man come upon him and whelm him,
    Embrace him and squeeze him, *'recite!'*
This embrace was a strengthening, readying for
    Revelation that would nigh descend.
By the majesty of the *tawajjuh*,[43] the Prophet was awed,
    Asked, *'what shall I recite?'*

And once more did the man come upon him and whelm him,
    Embrace him and squeeze him: *'Recite!*
In the name of your Lord who created; created
    All men from a seed like a clot,
Recite! for your Lord is Most Bountiful; taught
    By the Pen; taught man what he knew not.' [44]

| Recite al-'Alaq: 1-5 |

بِسْمِ ٱللَّهِ ٱلرَّحْمَٰنِ ٱلرَّحِيمِ

ٱقْرَأْ بِٱسْمِ رَبِّكَ ٱلَّذِى خَلَقَ ۞ خَلَقَ ٱلْإِنسَٰنَ مِنْ عَلَقٍ ۞ ٱقْرَأْ وَرَبُّكَ ٱلْأَكْرَمُ ۞ ٱلَّذِى عَلَّمَ بِٱلْقَلَمِ ۞ عَلَّمَ ٱلْإِنسَٰنَ مَا لَمْ يَعْلَمْ

The Prophet recited as if this Recital was
    Written on his purest heart!
Overcome by the sheer magnificence, from Hira's
    Bosom he rushed to depart.
'You are Messenger of Allah, I am Gibril!'

---

43 *tawajjuh*: spiritual transference – a term used by the Sufis to entail the transferral of heart-to-heart knowledge and spirituality, as discussed by Dihlawi in his Tafsir.
44 It is only once Gibril commanded him to recite *'by the name of your Lord'* that the Prophet was able to fully receive the overwheming puissance of revelation, and so began to recite, as described in a number of the commentaries on this hadith, including Bahjat al-Nufus.

Called the angel – for angel was he!
And then heavenwards did our Messenger gaze and
  Gibril did encompass the west
And the east and the north and the south; each horizon
  Astride, his great wings spread abreast!

So the Seal of the Messengers hastened away
  To his home where Khadijah did wait,
And he cried, *'cover me! cover me!'* and she held him
  Until all his awe did abate.
His heart quaking, he shared his great Message – divine awe
  And terror a-pound in his heart.

'I do fear for myself,' for he knew it was Truth –
  How tremendous a truth to impart!
What a virtuous wife! Ever-faithful Khadijah!
  Ne'er once did she doubt what he said!
*'Who but you could be Chosen? Great-hearted
  Protector of widows and orphans?'* she said.

Hear of Waraqah, cousin of her's, of the few
  Hunafa: Christians in the Vale,
Who awaited the Prophet foretold in their Scriptures;
  And, verily, now 'twas unveiled!
*'Dear cousin, in truth! You are he long foretold;
  The last Messenger willed for this land,
Rest assured, and prepare, for your own will deny;
  If I live, by your side, will I stand!'*

THERE WAS silence a while,[45] in which Waraqah died,
  And the Prophet did wait in despair

---

45 This is known as the 'revelatory pause' (*fatrat al-wahi*), whose length is disputed by the scholars, with estimates ranging from forty days to three years.

An Original English Mawlid

That Allah was displeased and withheld revelation;
    He turned to the Cave, waiting there.
Then, at last, as he walked in the wilderness, saw he
    Gibril 'twixt the heavens and earth,
His pure splendour surrounding, his glory resounding:
    He spoke to the Prophet these words:

'Truly, I am Gibril, you are God's Messenger!' And again
    Was He Taught by God seized
By the grandeur and brilliance of the Arch Angel
    Reciting, and he was relieved.
From Allah's greatest oceans of knowledge and bounty
    And plenitude was this revealed:[46]

'**N**ŪN!
    By the Pen and that which they inscribe;
        By the grace of your Lord, you are not
Covered over in spirit[47] *- behold that for you are rewards,*
        Close at hand, beyond count!
And I truly do swear - and again do I swear! –
        By My majesty and by My grace
That you have, O Muhammad, attained the perfection
        Of every ennobling state!

And you soon will perceive, as they too shall perceive,
        Which of you is afflicted, astray;

---

46 There is a significant difference of opinion about the second revelation, based on the various narrations regarding it. The most famous opinion is that the second revelation was *al-Muddathir* 1:5, based on the hadith of Jabir ibn Abdillah, whilst another opinion was affirms that it was *al-Duha*, which specifically addresses the Prophet's ﷺ despair about the pause in revelation. The position stated here is mentioned in 'Ayni's *Umdat al-Qari* (1:142), which has the further benefit of mentioning Allah's praise of the Prophet's ﷺ lofty character.
47 *Majnun* is often translated as 'insane', which is contextually correct as a direct response to the idolators who declared him as such, and is the meaning adopted by most commentators. However, it does not convey the full linguistic sense of the word *majnun*, which means 'to be covered.' In this instance, as discussed by Siraj al-Halabi, it also entails *'you are neither a man possessed nor one covered over in spirit'* – that is, your spirituality is unrestricted.

THE SOLILOQUY OF THE FULL MOON

*For Allah knoweth better which soul has been guided
And which is misled from His way.'*

| Recite al-Qalam 1-7 |

بِسْمِ ٱللَّهِ ٱلرَّحْمَٰنِ ٱلرَّحِيمِ

نٓ وَٱلْقَلَمِ وَمَا يَسْطُرُونَ ۞ مَآ أَنتَ بِنِعْمَةِ رَبِّكَ بِمَجْنُونٍ ۞ وَإِنَّ لَكَ لَأَجْرًا غَيْرَ مَمْنُونٍ ۞ وَإِنَّكَ لَعَلَىٰ خُلُقٍ عَظِيمٍ ۞ فَسَتُبْصِرُ وَيُبْصِرُونَ ۞ بِأَييِّكُمُ ٱلْمَفْتُونُ ۞ إِنَّ رَبَّكَ هُوَ أَعْلَمُ بِمَن ضَلَّ عَن سَبِيلِهِۦ وَهُوَ أَعْلَمُ بِٱلْمُهْتَدِينَ

O Lord Most High, do sanctify the one Prophetic Seal,
And with your grace, perfume the place his blessed form conceals.
And elevate and consecrate and hallow ever more
Madinah's earth, Jerusalem, and blessed Umm al-Qura,
Exalting he whose sandal made them pure.

An Original English Mawlid

الفصل الثامن

⟶ THE NIGHT JOURNEY ⟵

In which is described the last splitting of the Prophet's ﷺ blessed chest, the journey by night to Jerusalem, his leadership of the Prophets ﷺ in prayer, and their supplications of thanks.

Iambic Heptameter

TEN YEARS had passed since revelation in the Cave appeared
As light had spread, within that time, so too had darkness reared
Amassing as the disbelievers tortured and maligned
And struck the Muslims with their sword of endless woe and trial.

The Prophet and companions were driven from their land
Exiled to mountain, starved, forsaken; cast from Makkan sand.
Eight years since first he'd stood atop Abu Qubays and called –
The Truthful, they had called him, till they heard the Truth he spoke!

الصَّادِق

The faithful then had followed him, the others had decried[48]
They had belied[49] – they turned away – his message, they denied.
There now befell the hardest year, the year of grief and strife,
For lost to him, his strength, his comforter, his ardent wife.
Khadijah Great, the first to answer his Prophetic call -
Of boundless faith was she; to exile's hardship did she fall.

And Abu Talib who had raised the Prophet in his home
Did pass; the Prophet mourned him who had loved him as his own.

---
48 *decry*: to condemn or mock
49 *belie*: to declare something a lie or misrepresent

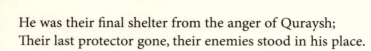 THE SOLILOQUY OF THE FULL MOON

He was their final shelter from the anger of Quraysh;
Their last protector gone, their enemies stood in his place.

WITHIN the Hijr, at the House, the Prophet was asleep
Beneath a waning crescent, when, descending at his feet
Alighted three archangels great: the first of them Gibril;
The Ward of Revelation and, behind him, Mika'il;
The Ward of earthly sustenance; the third was Israfil,
The Angel of the Trumpet had not once awayed his stand
Since starless age till time be lost not once was he relieved
Except to greet the Messenger upon this wedding eve.[50]

They laid him on the earth and filled a bowl with Zamzam's spring
'That we may purify your heart and then expand your breast.'
And this they did, and washed it thrice. A golden vessel next
Was brought, a-brim with wisdom which they emptied in his chest.
They closed it at his shoulder blades upon the Prophet's Seal,
So certainty and knowledge were within his heart unsealed.

They brought him by a bridled steed who bore a handsome face,
Buraq, whose stride reached till the farthest point within his gaze.
Gibril, he took the stirrup; Mika'il, he took the reins.
The Prophet mounted and they travelled far from Makkah's vale.

'Alight and pray,' Gibril did say; a wellspring they had reached.
'This is Tayba: the land where the Migration will surcease.'

'Alight and pray,' Gibril did say; a second time they ceased.
'This is Madyan where Moses found, on fleeing Pharoah, peace.'

'Alight and pray,' Gibril did say; a third time did they rest.
'This mount is Sinai whence your Lord held Moses in address.'

'Alight and pray,' Gibril did say; a final time, they paused.
'Here: Bethlehem, where Jesus son of Mariam was born.'

---

50 'Wedding eve' here refers to the imminent meeting with God—an *'urs* as per the hadith

An Original English Mawlid

And so they went, in lightning flight, and wondrous sights they passed
Of feár and of splendour, till Jerusalem at last.
The Prophet then beheld before his eyes the Hallowed House
Upon its gate, as each of his forebears, he tied his mount.
He entered where the sun and moon were seen as they would set
And prayed, but tarried not, for soon a host had gathered there.

The Prophet saw, surrounding him, a kingly crowd of men
Of shining countenance – and then from heaven did descend
A concourse bright of seraphim, and all did rise and stand:
Came every Prophet, every Messenger from every land.

They formed the lines of congregation and they bowed their heads;
Gibril then took the Prophet's hand – by him they would be led.
The angel raised the call to prayer, the Prophet did attend;
This Fellowship Divine did every brilliance transcend!
In God's great name was their commencement and in peace their end.

They glorified their Lord Exalted. Abraham then said:
    'All praise to God Almighty, He
        Who took me as His cherished friend,
    Who gave to my community
        The one by whom the prayer is led,
    Who cooled the flame and rescued me
        From Nimrod's ire and evil end.'

> All Prophetic du'as are in octameters; the introductory lines are **heptameters**

They magnified their Lord Exalted, Moses prayed and said:
    'All praise to God Almighty, He
        Who took me in direct address,
    By Whom the Pharaoh was destroyed,
        And Israel's Children safeguarded,
    Who brought from my community
        A truthful folk of righteousness.'

THE SOLILOQUY OF THE FULL MOON

They sanctified their Lord Exalted, David prayed and said:
'All praise to God Almighty who
    Has brought to me a kingdom great,
Who softened iron and gave to me
    The lauding bird and mountain's weight,
Who gave to me distinguished judgement
    And by wisdom raised my state.'

They elevated God Exalted, Solomon then said:
'All praise to God Almighty for
    The winds and jinn at my request,
Who granted knowledge and dominion –
    Ne'er again its like is set,
Who blessed with goodly kingdom;
    Never reckoning nor penance met.'

They hymned the praise of God Exalted, Jesus Christ then said:
'All praise to God Almighty Who
    Has made me as His blessed Word,
Who through me taught the Book, Evangel;
    Healed the blind and raised the dead,
Who raised me and my mother, and
    Did guard us from the Devil's stead.

And all did hallow God Exalted. Then our Prophet said,
'Praise to Allah who sent me as
    A Mercy unto every world;
Sent me a *bearer of glad tidings*
    And a *warner to the earth;*
Who, on my shoulders and my heart,
    His blessed Word made to descend
Within its exposition lies
    The perfect truth until all ends;
Who made my people median,
    Raised up to benefit mankind:

رحمة للعالمين

بشير

نذير

    The first that Paradise shall welcome,
        And the last the earth shall find;
    My breast expanded, burden lifted,
        Name exalted, station granted.'[51]

Hence the Prophets honoured him until the Messenger departed.

    Glorious is He who took His
        Servant from the Sacred House
    By night unto the Sacred Precincts
        Whose surroundings We have blessed
    To show him of Our signs; indeed
        He is the Hearing and the Seeing.

    | Recite Surah al-Isra: 1|

بِسْمِ ٱللَّهِ ٱلرَّحْمَٰنِ ٱلرَّحِيمِ

سُبْحَٰنَ ٱلَّذِىٓ أَسْرَىٰ بِعَبْدِهِۦ لَيْلًا مِّنَ ٱلْمَسْجِدِ ٱلْحَرَامِ إِلَى ٱلْمَسْجِدِ ٱلْأَقْصَا ٱلَّذِى بَٰرَكْنَا حَوْلَهُۥ لِنُرِيَهُۥ مِنْ ءَايَٰتِنَآ إِنَّهُۥ هُوَ ٱلسَّمِيعُ ٱلْبَصِيرُ

    O Lord Most High, do sanctify the one Prophetic Seal,
And with your grace, perfume the place his blessed form conceals.
    And elevate and consecrate and hallow ever more
    Madinah's earth, Jerusalem, and blessed Umm al-Qura,
    Exalting he whose sandal made them pure.

---

51 The last line being a reference to Sura al-Inshirah (*Alam nashrah laka sadraka...*)

الفَصْلُ التَّاسِعُ

── THE ASCENSION ──

In which is described the blessed Prophet's ﷺ sojourn through the seven heavens, his meetings with his Prophetic brethren, the entry into the Divine Presence, and the gifting of the prayer.

Iambic Octameter

A LADDER then to heaven rose,[52]
    For Adam's children to ascend
Bedecked with pearls and gilt in gold,
    And angels lining right and left.
They reached the nearest firmament;
    'Who goes there?' called its sentry thence.
'Gibril!' – 'And with you?' – ''Tis Muhammad' –
    'Welcome, from your kindred, hence!'

Within its breadth, the father of all men beheld the Messenger.
To shining halls of *Illiyin*[53] did Adam send his offspring graced;
While to the lowly *Sijjin* fells, awayed were those of shadowed face.
The Prophet gave his father greeting, and his greeting was returned.
'A welcome to a righteous Prophet! Welcome to a righteous son!'

On through yon firmaments they went;
    'Who goes there?' called the sentries thence.

---

52 This chapter is derived largely from two works entitled *al-Isra wa al-Miraj* by al-Salihi and al-'Alawi, which collate, critique and structure the numerous hadiths on the subject.
53 *Illiyun* and *Sijjin* are the abodes of the righteous and unrighteous (or believers and disbelievers) in the *Barzakh*: one expansive and lofty in the seventh heaven, the other narrow and constricted beneath the seventh earth, as mentioned by Ibn Kathir in his Tafsir.

THE SOLILOQUY OF THE FULL MOON

'Gibril!' – 'And with you?' – 'Tis Muhammad' –
'Welcome, from your kindred, hence!'

Stood in the second lofty sky two men alike of mien[54] and form:
'Isa the son of Mariam, and Yahya, Zakariyya's son,
Of roseate face and curling tress, returning greeting with address:
'A welcome to a righteous brother! On a righteous Prophet peace!'

So went they on, ascending high, and such did every Prophet cry.
The splendour of the heaven third did pale to ether as was seen
Moonfairness shine on Yusuf's brow – *'upon a righteous Prophet peace!'*
And for the fourth, there stood Idris, beside the books of earthly deeds.
August and reverenced was he – *'upon a righteous Prophet peace!'*

The fifth: where stood a bearded man of downy white and ebony;[55]
Harun, beloved of his folk – *'upon a righteous Prophet peace!'*
The sixth did see a gathering collected in its haven fair.
But when the Prophet raised his eyes, he saw across the twilit skies –
In image of his fellowship – a greater throng assembled there.

Within that place, a mighty man of russet face and sturdy stand;
Whose hair was rife upon his head, and chin, and chest, and arm
                                                       and hand.
But when the Prophet went to him the strong and stalwart Musa wept,
'That one who has come after me has called more souls unto the truth.
Most-honoured, such they call me, yet more-honoured still are you, in sooth!
A welcome to a righteous brother! On a righteous Prophet peace!'

And finally the seventh sky! A throne engilded, lofty, leant
Upon the House Inhabited[56] by angels, in their praise content.
Arrayed therein a company, irradiant, magnificent;

---
54 *mien*: bearing and deportment
55 The beard of Harun was described as 'salt and pepper' or 'half black and half white.'
56 *al-Bayt al-Ma'mur* – the Ka'bah of the heavens to which angels make pilgrimage

And regally, upon the chair, awaited Ibrahim the Friend.
'A welcome to a righteous Prophet! Welcome to a righteous son!
My greeting to your people and this message do convey afar:
The Garden's soil is excellent and water sweet. Its seedlings are
These words: 'All glory is to God; and praise is for Allah alone;
There is no God except Allah; most great is He – so seeds are sown.'[57]

STILL, far aloft beyond the spheres,
    The Prophet and Gibril were borne,
O'er wondrous lengths and leagues undreamed,
    Until he reached the farthest bound.
As unto timeless halls he went
    Where starlit leaves hung glimmering.
Then he beheld in tall ascent
    The Lote-Tree of the Utterest End
And was he thence but two bows' lengths
    From God's immortal majesty.

There, incandescent light did break,
    And hues a hundred colours glowed.
And from a trunk of endless height –
    Bestrewn with jewels – did rivers flow,
Of honey sweet and palest milk,
    And wine and water crystalline.
And at its roots, a vast sea lay
    Of musk – the source of Salsabil,
Whose shimm'ring billows roared and rolled
    At arrow's speed o'er pebbles bright.
And Kawthar! Paradise's fount –
    Its cooling drink is pure respite.
He took to drink beside its banks
    And saw he vessels, grey and golden;

---

57 ie: the dhikr of: سُبْحَانَ الله و الحَمْدُ لله و لا إلَهَ إلا الله و الله أكْبَرُ

THE SOLILOQUY OF THE FULL MOON

On its strand pavilions,
        With domes of hollowed pearl upholden.

And then Gibril did halt and say,
        'The Lote-Tree holds my hallowed niche,
And, at its bound, my station ends;
        The Lote-Tree is the farthest reach.
I dare not pass the final veil
        That yet remains; though I may yearn,
For should I step into the Light,
        Then, verily, my wings will burn!'

Gibril did falter, all did fail.
        The Prophet rose beyond the veil,
To hear the scribing of the quills,
        On tablets, God's eternal will.
Enshrouding clouds around concealed,
        As God Almighty was revealed.[58]

We silent stand; we say no more.
        A secret lay beyond that door.
And say we naught; if uttered aught,
        Then none but speech that He has wrought.
'No vision may encompass Him;
        For vision He encompasses.'

This quatrain is heptameter, before returning to octameter

There are no words by which we may that hallowed tryst describe.
No speech befits His countenance. No verses may we cry
In praise. For sight is sealed for us; no tongue to glorify.
What can be said when naught was said by him, alone, brought nigh?

---

58 The question of whether the Prophet ﷺ beheld God Almighty is one that has been debated from the very first generation, with Ibn 'Abbas affirming it and 'Aisha denying it. As for its manner, that is beyond human comprehension. Nawawi declared that the majority of scholars affirmed the Divine beholding. The author has chosen to remain silent about the nature of the Divine encounter in keeping with the allusiveness of the Quranic narrative.

~ **An Original English Mawlid** ~

'Yea! By the Star when it descends,
    Your bless'd companion has not strayed,
Nor has he erred or been deceived,
    Nor does he speak from his desire.
And it is naught but Lordly revelation
    That has been inspired.'
'And at the Lote of Utmost Bound
    Nigh to the Garden of Abode
And lo! The Lote-Tree is enshrouded
    By that which does there enshroud.
The eye and sight turned not away,
    Nor did transgress, ne'er yet was bold.
And verily he saw the greatest
    Revelations of his Lord.'

| Recite Surah al-Najm: 1-18 |

وَٱلنَّجْمِ إِذَا هَوَىٰ ۞ مَا ضَلَّ صَاحِبُكُمْ وَمَا غَوَىٰ ۞ وَمَا يَنطِقُ عَنِ ٱلْهَوَىٰ ۞ إِنْ هُوَ إِلَّا وَحْيٌ يُوحَىٰ ۞ عَلَّمَهُ شَدِيدُ ٱلْقُوَىٰ ۞ ذُو مِرَّةٍ فَٱسْتَوَىٰ ۞ وَهُوَ بِٱلْأُفُقِ ٱلْأَعْلَىٰ ۞ ثُمَّ دَنَا فَتَدَلَّىٰ ۞ فَكَانَ قَابَ قَوْسَيْنِ أَوْ أَدْنَىٰ ۞ فَأَوْحَىٰ إِلَىٰ عَبْدِهِ مَا أَوْحَىٰ ۞ مَا كَذَبَ ٱلْفُؤَادُ مَا رَأَىٰ ۞ أَفَتُمَارُونَهُ عَلَىٰ مَا يَرَىٰ ۞ وَلَقَدْ رَآهُ نَزْلَةً أُخْرَىٰ ۞ عِندَ سِدْرَةِ ٱلْمُنتَهَىٰ ۞ عِندَهَا جَنَّةُ ٱلْمَأْوَىٰ ۞ إِذْ يَغْشَى ٱلسِّدْرَةَ مَا يَغْشَىٰ ۞ مَا زَاغَ ٱلْبَصَرُ وَمَا طَغَىٰ ۞ لَقَدْ رَأَىٰ مِنْ ءَايَـٰتِ رَبِّهِ ٱلْكُبْرَىٰ ۞

The awestruck angel silence kept
    All through the firmaments' decline

THE SOLILOQUY OF THE FULL MOON

So 'twas till Musa called the Prophet,
    'Tell me of my Lord Divine.'
For love had grasped our Musa's heart,
    As saw he in the Prophet's eyes,
That which he'd asked so long ago
    Nine times to hold within his own.

Remembered he the mountain great,
    That shattered from *tajalli's* awe
Remembered he the forty days
    Spent thunderstruck before his Lord.
The Prophet told him of the gift -
    The fifty prayers that God ordained.
Said Musa, *'nay – the men are weak!*
    Return; a lighter task beseech.'
So went the Prophet back and forth
    Nine times until the prayers were five.
'Return!' said Musa. 'I cannot,'
    The Prophet said, 'I am too shy!'
So Musa's prayer, from ages past,
    Was nine times answered, nine times asked.
He'd longed to see Allah Most High;
    Allah was in Muhammad's eye!

O Lord Most High, do sanctify the one Prophetic Seal,
And with your grace, perfume the place his blessed form conceals.
And elevate and consecrate and hallow ever more
Madinah's earth, Jerusalem, and blessed Umm al-Qura,
Exalting he whose sandal made them pure.

An Original English Mawlid

QASIDA
THE ASCENSION

From the Sacred House to Jerusalem,
Through the seven heavens did he ascend
To the Love Divine beyond 'where' or 'when',
Send peace on him and his family!

| Refrain |

Balaghal ulā bi kamālihi
Kashafa ad-duja bi jamālihi
Hasunat jāmi'u khisālihi
Sallu alayhi wa ālihi

Like a moon set sail on the heaven's seas
Through the dark night riding on the lightning-steed.
See! One born of earth strides the heaven's fields!
Send peace on him and his family!
And the stars gave thanks and the moon did weep
As its beauty paled before the Hashimi
For what sun or moon can compare to him?
Send peace on him and his family!

| Refrain |

THE SOLILOQUY OF THE FULL MOON

As his heart was strengthened and purified,
And was filled with wisdom and light on light
So the wells of Zamzam he sanctified,
Send peace on him and his family!

And the Prophets – Adam to Jesus Christ –
Came to honour him and to pray behind
One from whose lamp they had received their light.
Send peace on him and his family!

| Refrain |

And the gates of heaven, so high and strong,
Opened joyfully for the one called upon
And the angels sang 'peace on you, welcome!'
Send peace on him and his family!

When Gibril did falter, Muhammad rose,
Where no Prophet nor angel may approach
So beloved to the Beloved returned!
Send peace on him and his family!

| Refrain |

For the peace that comes to surrendered hearts.
For the mercy descending when the prayer is called
For the blessings born of your charity.
Send peace on him and his family!

Through perfection did he attain the heights.
With his beauty did he dispel the night
Oh! How blessed are all of his qualities!
Send peace on him and his family!

| Refrain |

An Original English Mawlid

الفَصْلُ العَاشِرْ

∽ A PEN PORTRAIT ∽

In which are enumerated Shama'il al-Nabi – the beautiful outward qualities and features of the blessed Prophet ﷺ, as described by his companions.

Iambic Heptameter

HOW MANY times I've heard it, in my waxing and my wane,
His lovers and companions describing him and saying:
'Last night I looked upon the moon and then I looked at him;
In truth! The Prophet far surpassed the moon in radiance.'[59]

How many times I've heard as I have passed from east to west
The many calls for *hilya*[60] – count the lovers who have said,
'His countenance, the fullest moon! Resplendent, shining bright
Yet brighter than the full moon and its luminescent light.'[61]
Ne'er doubt he was irradiant; in times when he was pleased
His visage was a mirror bright, and *I* reflected *him*.[62]

منير

As one said, *'when his forehead does appear in darkest night
It shines and gleams so that none need their lanterns to ignite.'*[63]
In truth, the sun did never rise until he came to wake;
And if you saw him, verily, you saw the dawn light break![64]

---

59 Narrated by a number of companions, including Jabir ibn Samura in Tirmidhi
60 *Hilya* is the term for the verbal description of the Prophet ﷺ, such as his grandsons al-Hasan and al-Husayn asked for from their uncle Hind ibn Abi Hala in the Shama'il Tirmidhi
61 Such as Abu Bakr, Rubayy', Jabir, Ali and al-Hamdani, in Muslim, Tirmidhi, and others
62 Narrated by Abu Tufayl in Muslim
63 Part of a poem by Abu Bakr al-Siddiq
64 Rubayy' ibn Mu'awwadh in Tirmidhi and Bayhaqi

THE SOLILOQUY OF THE FULL MOON

So broad and smooth his brow, and alabaster were his cheeks;
Why! It was such that clouds themselves his fairest hue would seek.[65]
I wish that I had seen his eyes more often than I did,
For ever were they lowered - very rarely did he raise
His eyes, most humble, and the earth delighted in his gaze.[66]

I saw them, clarion, but twice – of deepest black were they,[67]
A gentle, reddish tint within their whites[68] – a full array
Of eyelashes; both naturally anointed and defined,
A-glance on things with gentleness – to subtlety inclined.[69]
These handsome eyes were crowned by brows: two arches, finely curved.[70]

Believe the poet when he says, *'these are the two bows' lengths;*
The furthest point, Qaba Qawsain, between them grandly rests.'
'His nose, an Alif, does the poet write, *'his eyebrows, Nūns!'* [71]
His nose was aquiline and elevated, finely hewn.
And every eloquence displayed upon his mouth and smile;
His teeth: spaced perfectly and bright, like lightning flashed inside.[72]

And from his purest tongue were blessed droplets all bequeathed
To quench, increase and grant with strength—how many were so healed![73]
A mother needn't nurse a child – his spittle would suffice;[74]
A blinded man's eye was restored and once much time had passed
That same eye saw with clarity – the other one was masked![75]

---

65 From the poem of Abu Talib related by Bayhaqi
66 The hadith of Hind ibn Abi Hala in Tirmidhi
67 Narrated by Ali in Tirmidhi
68 Narrated by Ali in Sahih Muslim and Bayhaqi
69 The hadith of Hind ibn Abi Hala in Tirmidhi
70 Narrated by Ali in Tirmidhi
71 All from Ahmad Rida Khan in his Qasida Nuriyya
72 All in Tirmidhi from different narrators
73 The narrations on this are too many to mention, such as Ali at Khaybar narrated in Bukhari
74 Narrated by al-Hasan in Tabarani
75 Abu Qatada narrates this about Ibn Qatada in Bayhaqi

An Original English Mawlid

His neck was smooth and ivory, a most desired length,
His shoulders, broad and stately, did display unrivalled strength.
Expansive, straight and levelled was his alabastrine[76] breast;
A single line of finest hair did grow upon his chest.
And see his back; though ever-bowing, it was never bent –
Prostration never ceased, and yet, his back in straight ascent!

His beard, dark and full and soft did envelop his chin
And ne'er a moment passed except a smile was wrapped within.[77]
His locks of hair were ebony cascading down his neck,[78]
As dark as night they gathered at his ears, with curls bedecked.[79]

Was ever known a child whose head, by him, had been caressed
For on their hair a sweetest perfume fragrantly did rest.[80]
They all did say, *'I have not smelt an ambergris or musk*
Of sweeter redolence than our Prophet's perfumed touch.'[81]
This fragrance came from his own hands, both cool, akin to ice[82]
A steadfast handhold, gentle, strong; their waters, pure respite![83]

In all, he was one median - not one could fault his height;[84]
Not short, nor one too tall; in company, the most upright.[85]
His feet so smooth and sloped that water drops could roll with ease.[86]
As for his stride, it was as if the earth did rush to meet
Him as he walked, although he never spurred or hastened step.
With ease he went, and yet his friends made haste to follow there![87]

---

76 *Alabastrine*: pertaining to the purity and colour of alabaster
77 Jabir in Bukhari and Muslim
78 All the above from the hadith of Hind and others in Tirmidhi
79 Aisha from Tirmidhi
80 Aisha in Bayhaqi and Abu Nu'aym
81 Anas ibn Malik from Muslim and Tirmidhi
82 Jabir ibn Samura in Muslim
83 A reference to the mutawatir hadith about water flowing from his blessed hands to quench the thirst of his companions – narrated in Bukhari and Muslim
84 Ali from Tirmidhi
85 Narrated in Bayhaqi
86 From the hadith of Hind ibn Abi Hala
87 Both from Abu Hurayra from Tirmidhi and Musnad Ahmad

THE SOLILOQUY OF THE FULL MOON

What brevity within his words whenever he did speak –
Yet held within them wisdom that encompassed everything![88]
Pure eloquence, his sentences so clear, ne'er idling,
But rare and precious, like as threaded pearls upon a string.[89]

What meeting of full majesty and mercy manifest
Within his person, formed with pure perfection, ever-blessed!
Whenever one did come to him, their heart would quake with fear
Until he eased their worry and became to them most dear.[90]
And all who stayed with him and saw the beauty of his heart
Did love him and believe in him, and wished to never part.[91]

Heed Ali's words when he said, *'there was never one akin
That I did see, of fairer face, before or after him.'* [92]

O Lord Most High, do sanctify the one Prophetic Seal,
And with your grace, perfume the place his blessed form conceals.
And elevate and consecrate and hallow ever more
Madinah's earth, Jerusalem, and blessed Umm al-Qura,
Exalting he whose sandal made them pure.

---

88 Abu Hurayra from Bukhari - *'I have been sent with encompassing speech.'*
89 Aisha from Bukhari
90 Bukhari also narrates that a man came to him and was awestruck, until the Prophet ﷺ spoke to him and allayed his fear. Similar is reported by Qayla bint Makhrama.
91 Ali from Tirmidhi: *'whoever came upon him him unexpectedly was in awe of him; whoever stayed with him fell in love with him.'*
92 Reported by a number of companions, including Ali in Tirmidhi

QASIDA
HILYAT AL-NABI

| Refrain |

Balaghal ulā bi kamālihi
Kashafa ad-duja bi jamālihi
Hasunat jāmi'u khisālihi
Sallu alayhi wa ālihi

For his face, that shone like the sun and moon;
For his smile, that lightened a darkened room;
For his life, that turned night to brightest noon:
Send peace on him and his family.

As his hands brought fragrance to all they touched
With a perfume sweeter than rose or musk,
His remembrance perfumes the dawn and dusk!
Send peace on him and his family.

| Refrain |

For his hair, that shone ebony and black,
That like streams cascaded towards his neck,
For the seal of prophecy upon his back:
Send peace on him and his family.

THE SOLILOQUY OF THE FULL MOON

For his teeth, that shone with a diamond's gleam;
For his neck, like silver and ivory;
For his wisdom, priceless beyond all things:
Send peace on him and his family.

| Refrain |

For his hands that toiled, yet were smooth and soft;
For his feet that swelled as he worshipped God;
For the marks on his back that brought tears to Umar:
Send peace on him and his family

When his blessed body was pierced by rocks,
With blood streaming forth, he gave this response:
'Oh Allah, forgive them, for they know not!'
Send peace on him and his family.

| Refrain |

For his name is Ahmad and Muhammad.
He is praised in heaven and praised on earth –
Though no praise can reach to his true worth! –
Send peace on him and his family.

All who came to him were in awe of him;
All who stayed with him fell in love with him.
Oh! How fortunate to have been one of them!
Send peace on him and his family.

| Refrain |

An Original English Mawlid

الفَصْلُ الحَادِي عَشَرَ

HIS EXALTED CHARACTER

In which is described something of the superlative character and qualities of the Best of Creation ﷺ, particularly his being a manifestation of pure mercy.

Iambic Heptameter

YOU CANNOT know the secret truth of his most perfect heart!
These few words of description fade away when held to him;
His beauty was but a reflection of his inward state –
A character so lofty that *unjustly* I narrate.

Perhaps you wonder why I have spent time to illustrate
His countenance and beauty? Well! what lover does not yearn
To know of their beloved, see his visage in their eyes?
And now you see him: fall in love with his spirit sublime!

He ever was the greatest Mercy sent unto the worlds![93]
No man or woman came upon him except that they left
In gladness at his goodness, with their hearts and minds content.[94]

No beggar or a Bedouin who came with empty packs
Did leave without whatever he possessed upon their backs![95]
No child did pass except they laughed in mirth and merriment

---

93 *'We sent you not but as a mercy to all the worlds'* – Anbiya (21:107)
94 Narrated in Nasa'i
95 Hadiths of this sort are so numerous as to be mutawatir

THE SOLILOQUY OF THE FULL MOON

And played with him[96] – some climbed on him![97] – and were
                                         perfumed with scent.
The mere grains of soil and sand did find with him respite:
'The servants of the Merciful, upon the earth, tread light.' [98]

Has news reached you about the bird who unto him complained,
Lamenting of her stolen eggs, in anguished woe and pain?
For her, into the desert, he set out to them regain.[99]

And have you heard of how, in battle's march, he came across
A mother with her pups. Concerned that she'd not be distraught
Or fearful, he stationed guards and changed his army's course![100]
Or of the camel, so mistreated, who did come to weep;
The Prophet called its owner saying, *'this camel that you keep
Is from Allah, so fear Him, and cause this beast no grief!'*[101]

His way with all creation was as one not touched by need,
Yet when he stood before his Lord no other would he heed.[102]
He passed his nights in penitent devotion, lost in prayer
Until his feet would swell and crack. When he was made aware
And asked why one so pure and sinless felt such need to plead
And weep, he answered, *'should I not a thankful servant be?"* [103]
In truth, his tears and sorrowful concern was for mankind
That they might live in peace in this world and at end of times.[104]

When hope seemed lost, and all ways blocked, his faith would never fail.
He'd place his trust in God alone; when cornered in the cave,
Beset by foes, he said, to still his friend's concern, *'Don't grieve!*

---

96 'The Prophet ﷺ would sometimes line up the children and make them race to him, hugging and kissing them when they came – Sahih Ibn Hibban
97 Such as his grandchildren: al-Hasan, al-Husayn and Umamah, also see al-Shifa of 'Iyad
98 Al-Furqan (25:63)
99 Abu Dawud
100 Maghazi al-Waqidi
101 Narrated by Abu Dawud
102 Paraphrased from Ibn 'Ataillah: *'be with people like one who has no nafs, and be with God like one for whom nothing else exists.'*
103 Narrated by Aisha in Bukhari
104 Bukhari: *'I am trying to pull you from the Fire, but you keep rushing headlong towards it.'*

Not two are we, for God is with us!' – thus descended peace.¹⁰⁵

And when 'twas time to stand his ground, his valour knew no peer;
Where battle fiercest raged, the brave would shelter seek with him.¹⁰⁶
He needed neither sword nor spear – mere dust would turn the tide
When cast from hand of him who fought with angels by his side!¹⁰⁷
Yet when the victory was at hand, the conquered found that he
Was both the Messenger of Battle and of Clemency.¹⁰⁸

رسول الملاحم

If one held out their hand to him, his hand he'd not refuse,
Nor would he then withdraw until themselves they would excuse.¹⁰⁹
How honoured were his fellowship! He made them feel at ease.
He'd sit amongst them and they would converse on what they pleased.
These bless'd companions weren't repressed, and never were they harsh;
Together, they'd sing poetry with him, they'd joke and laugh.¹¹⁰

رسول الرحمة

Relaxed and spreading joy, the Ever-Smiling was his name,¹¹¹
That followers may learn his ways, good character attain.
He would not dominate in speech, or interrupt affairs,¹¹²
But when he spoke, no other spoke, all listening with care.
'Twas said by them, *'the Prophet of Allah did never greet
Or speak except he smiled, embracing us, when we did meet.'* ¹¹³

الضّحّاك

He ever was Concerned for his community and friends.¹¹⁴
Whenever a companion was absent he would ask
Of his wellbeing and visit him;¹¹⁵ and in the times of night,
He'd miss these friends and listen for Quran that they'd recite. ¹¹⁶

عزيز عليه

---

105 Al-Tauba (9:40)
106 From Bara' ibn 'Azib in Muslim and 'Ali in Musnad Ahmad, both regarding Hunayn
107 al-Anfal (8:17) and its commentaries – also a continuation of the above hadiths
108 Examples to numerous to recount, including Makkah, Hunayn, Badr, Mustaliq, etc
109 Narrated by Bazzar and Tabarani
110 Kharija ibn Zayd from Tirmidhi and Jabir ibn Samura from Muslim respectively
111 Abu Darda from Musnad Ahmad - *al-Dahhak* was this name
112 Kharija ibn Zayd from Abu Dawud
113 See previous references
114 As mentioned in the Quran – Sura Tauba (9:128)
115 From the hadith of Hind in Tirmidhi, as well as Anas in Musnad Abi Ya'la
116 Narrated in Sayyiduna Muhammad Rasulullah of Siraj al-Halabi

THE SOLILOQUY OF THE FULL MOON

There was not one more just than him – and greater still was he,
When one was just to him, he'd answer more excellently![117]

Most patient was he, verily! And filled with taintless hope
At Ta'if, stoned and bleeding, when he sought to grant relief: .
The angels would have caused the mountains crush the land beneath!
But said he, *'nay! Perhaps shall come an offspring of belief.'*[118]

So know his outward form was but mirror-glass reflecting
An inner beauty of perfection, widely radiating;
And in this may I call a claim! For I am but a glass
That holds upon its clear face the light of one who was
The height of every brilliance whom no-one did surpass,
In mercy or in majesty or beauty of the heart.

And so may you, by this remembrance, burnish[119] rusted heart.
By love of him, do sanctify your soul and make it shine
That you may hold the faintest scintilla[120] of Light Divine.

O Lord Most High, do sanctify the one Prophetic Seal,
And with your grace, perfume the place his blessed form conceals.
And elevate and consecrate and hallow ever more
Madinah's earth, Jerusalem, and blessed Umm al-Qura,
Exalting he whose sandal made them pure.

---

117 Ibn Abbas from Bukhari and Muslim
118 A reference to the abuse suffered by the Prophet ﷺ at Ta'if and his response to the threat of angelic retribution upon them, as mentioned in Subul al-Huda wa al-Rashad
119 *burnish*: polish and adorn
120 *scintilla*: glimmer

An Original English Mawlid

QASIDA
O YOU TO WHOM THE BIRD COMPLAINED

THE SOLILOQUY OF THE FULL MOON

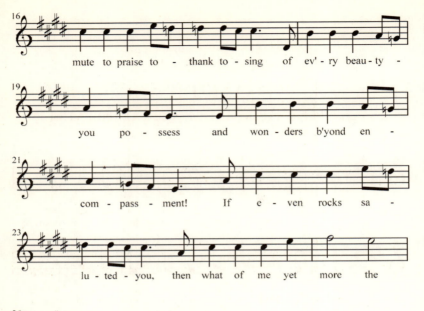

| Refrain |

*Salli ya Rabbi wa sallim ʿala al-Nabi Muhammadin
Shafiʿuna Habibuna wa alihi wa sahbihi*

O You to whom the bird complained,
Lamenting separation's pain;
O You for whom a blessed tree
Did bend its boughs to shelter thee.

An Original English Mawlid

| Refrain |

O You for whom the lizard stood,
Proclaiming clear your Prophethood;
O You for whose love withered trunks
Did come to life to seek your touch

And yet I stand, of human form –
Creation's pride before my fall –
Possessed of speech beyond all things
Yet mute to praise, to thank, to sing

Of every beauty you possess
And wonders beyond encompassment!
If even rocks saluted you,
Then what of me, yet more the fool?

| Refrain |

So why then should I not lament
My distance from immortal friend?
Or scorn to stand and celebrate
Whose intercession rules my fate?

| Refrain |

Or bend this form so full of pride
Before that place where you reside?
Or seek to raise this withered heart
To life immortal through your love?

O Lord! Let loose this knotted tongue
To sing the praise of th' chosen one!
Set free these hardened eyes to weep
Lamenting separation's grief

❧ THE SOLILOQUY OF THE FULL MOON ❧

Let every breath of mine expend
In benediction of the friend
And let this heart be purified
By love of him, till end of time.

| Refrain |

Note: this qasida can also be sung according to any of the tunes of the Qasida Burda, with the substitution of the long foot (*madd*) with a doubled note, as follows:

Maw-la- ya - sal - - li - wa - sal-lim - da-i-man - - a-ba-dan
So - why - then - should - I - not - la-ment - my - se-pa-ra-tion - from - the - friend?

An Original English Mawlid

الفَصْلُ الثَّانِي عَشَرَ

EPILOGUE

In which the Soliloquy of the Full Moon draws to a close with a description of the relationship between the believer and the Prophet ﷺ, and the author responds with a final supplication.

Iambic Heptameter

AND NOW my tale is almost done, for soon the sun shall rise,
On this bless'd night that hailed his birth, unveiled his
                                              dazzling light.
We have rejoiced in gladness, celebrating his advent,
Delighting in remembrance … yet still do I lament
For loneliness; I tremble in address, my tears fall.
I wonder when we'll meet again, or if we will at all?
I long have rued my silence at the gathering of souls,
Whence every being was summoned ere the worlds or deeds had
                                              passed;
Would that this covenant were made again, this mighty task
And I did know this Prophet's truth when God Almighty called,
'What taker?' then I swear, I would have said, 'it will be I!'
If I had known, eternally, I might stand by the side
Of him, the greatest Prophet, I'd have said, 'it will be I!'

We had our time, a precious time, and now the earth delights
In his most blessed presence, witnessing his blessed light.
But pity him who says, 'he long has gone, we are deprived.'
By God Most High, I swear that you, Muhammad, are alive!

THE SOLILOQUY OF THE FULL MOON

This is the truth, I do attest when God Exalted said,
*'If We had sent down this Quran upon a mountain great,
For awe of God you would have seen it struck asunder, rent!'* [121]

And as for him who held this same Quran within his heart?
Lo! When he turned his gaze on me, in awe I split apart
In twain. At his great majesty, thus riven did I fall!
And only by his love and mercy was I then restored.

Indeed, this awe is great, it splits the stubborn heart in two,
That every kindness, mercy, enters, sanctifying and through
This Light Divine, Prophetic love, the heart is formed anew.
And now I fall to silence, verily my tongue runs dry.
I speak no more; I've given all except my love inside.'

O blessed Moon! You've spoken true, and hence I do attest
That your sincere words of love have settled in my breast.
As you who were his company in earth and heaven set,
I turn my face to God who granted you a voice to speak,
In benediction, supplicating Him, do I beseech:

Iambic Octameter
⌣ ╱

Allah! Creator of the worlds;
    Omniscient; Omnipotent;
Most Merciful; Most Gracious;
    The Protecting Friend, Beneficent;

I ask, an abject slave before You,
    For your mercy – I implore You

These four lines only are Trochaic
╱ ⌣

That You graciously forgive us,
    All creation, all believers;
That You grant us ease, respite –
    Hereafter and in earthly life;

---

121 al-Hashr (59:21)

An Original English Mawlid

Accept our every plea and praise;
    Exalt our stations, ever raise
Our goodness and our love for You;
    Our worship, our servitude.

And make his countenance our guiding
    Lantern as we fare these ways;
And make his words our sentences,
    His litanies the prayers we pray;

And make his practice our actions,
    Echoes of his signal deeds;
And as his mind and heart were ever
    Wakeful, make us those who heed;
Remembering and worshipping and
    Bound to You alone, adoring;
And beseeching and entreating
    You, Sufficient One, imploring;

By him whom you love so dearly,
    Make us lovers, seeing clearly
Every truth that you've revealed;
    And those for whom he intercedes,

When fires of Hell leap up before us,
    Flames aflight in hungry chorus,
May he turn it on its heel
    And us beneath his cloak conceal.
Though darkness overlooms our souls,
    Make ours among the hands he holds;

May Halls of Bliss be our abode –
    Midst gardens 'neath which rivers flow –

THE SOLILOQUY OF THE FULL MOON

Among the goodly fellowship
    Of prophets, martyrs, and the true,
Who from his hands raise to their lips
    A draught that life and peace renews.

So ends this rhyme with praise of You,
    Remembrance and gratitude.
We seek your Countenance Divine
    Through love for him till end of time:
So may we never be apart from
    Him possessed of purest heart!

O Lord Most High, do sanctify the one Prophetic Seal,
And with your grace, perfume the place his blessed form conceals.
And elevate and consecrate and hallow ever more
Madinah's earth, Jerusalem, and blessed Umm al-Qura,
Exalting he whose sandal made them pure.

O Prophet, do accept from us our endless love for thee,
O Prophet, do accept from us this Light's Soliloquy.

An Original English Mawlid

✧ LOVE'S HARVEST ✧
On the Spirituality and Psychology of Mawlid

An Appendix by Talib al-Habib

*Come! We shall spread the perfume of love
In remembrance of the Elect of God.*

It is the nature of perfume to diffuse. A rose does not withhold its fragrance, but lets the wind to carry it wherever it will. So too, it is the nature of love – and the joyfulness that is born from it – to disseminate itself, that all who wander into its path may be refreshed and uplifted. This is not something that either the rose or the lover may consciously do – nor even prevent from happening – rather it is as natural as water's flowing downhill. In reality, this love is both the spiritual wellspring of the Muslim impulse to celebrate the *mawlid*, as well as its ultimate purpose.

Love, gratitude and joyfulness are not emotions that a person may easily contain within their breast. So it is perhaps inevitable that Muslims whose hearts overflow in love and thankfulness for the advent of Allah's greatest blessing ﷺ upon His creation, would wish to share their joy, to gather together in praise and remembrance; to celebrate and invite others to their celebration.

It is probable that, as you read this, somewhere around Allah's wide earth someone is making mawlid for of the best of creation, the

THE SOLILOQUY OF THE FULL MOON

blessed and beloved chosen of Allah, Sayyidina Muhammad ﷺ. The Holy Quran declares: *'Say! In the bounty of Allah and His mercy – in that let them rejoice. It is better than all that they gather to themselves.'* For centuries, Muslims have considered that there is no greater bounty, and no greater mercy, that Allah has favoured his creation with than the beloved Prophet ﷺ.

Gatherings in which Muslims come together have many spiritual advantages. A single fire gives more light than a hundred candles, and the same wind that will extinguish the latter will only fuel the former. In much the same way, a congregation of believers is stronger than solitary believers. Weak faith is strengthened by the presence of like-minded men and women, and one is encouraged and inspired by the actions of others. Allah says: *'help one another in piety and righteousness.'* This, of course, is the case for any Islamic gathering, as is the fact that they all revolve around Rasulullah ﷺ in some way. What, then, is so special about the *mawlid*?

Mawlid – The Psychology of Love

The study of the blessed Prophet ﷺ has many aspects. He is the inward root and outward trunk of the entire religion in a way that no other human being can claim to be. The study of *fiqh* may be viewed as the systematisation of his outward actions; *aqida*, his exposition of ultimate reality; *tasawwuf*, his character, personality and inward state. One may study his life-history (*sira*), his battles (*maghazi*), his habits, description and conduct (*shama'il*). One cannot but benefit from any and all of these types of study; and any Islamic gathering will tend to concentrate on one or more of them.

Mawlid specifically tends to focus the participants' attention on three aspects: his superlative qualities (*khasa'is*), his birth (*milad*), and singing his praise (*qasa'id*). Psychologically, these three aspects form a powerful synergy that ultimately inspires love for Rasulullah ﷺ.

The last-mentioned – the *qasa'id* or *na'at* that are an invariable feature of *mawlid* gatherings – utilise the beauty of poetic language and the human voice to melt the soul's resistance, arouse powerful emotions and create an opening (*fath*) in the heart. It is into this opening that the message contained in the first two aspects is poured.

Commemoration of his superlative qualities emphasises to the listener that it is no ordinary person being discussed – Rasulullah ﷺ was not only a man whose life was surrounded by miracles, but who was, in his essence, a living, breathing miracle. Wonder awakens: awe at his greatness, humility in contemplation of our own state, and thankfulness for Allah's blessing upon us. The heart is instilled with a sense of reverence, spiritually beholding the one for whose sake universes were created.

This veneration is, however, finely counter-balanced by the second aspect – the mention of his blessed birth. It reminds the reader of his earliest, most vulnerable period – of how the one before whom temporal kings are but dust came into this world an orphan. It reminds us of the ways he *is* like us; not an arch-angel, not some untouchable superhuman, but a human being born of woman and grown from a child. It humanises him, creating an intuitive bond between this legendary, supra-human entity and ordinary, fallible mortals.

This is why we love him in a way that we would not love the angel Gabriel, or a scripture, or an amorphous concept. The human soul inclines towards human souls; hearts connect to him through his manifest human nature (*bashariyya*), and through the crucible of his hidden spiritual luminosity (*nuraniyya*) are transformed and connected to their Lord. And within this mysterious connection between one heart and another is love found.

The great triumph of mawlid, which explains its continuing success and perpetuation over a millennium, is this ability to transcend the outward aspects of his actions, words and verdicts to unveil something of what he was in essence. The former, his characteristics, speak to our minds; but the latter speaks to our hearts. For one may admire, honour and incline towards a person because of their characteristics, but one loves a person because of their essence.

The Spring of Love

Thus the ultimate purpose and effect of mawlid gatherings – that which differentiates them from others – is their concentrated emphasis on developing, nurturing and sustaining love for Rasulullah ﷺ. Love is a mysterious, incomprehensible, potent force; it is the spring of vitality that moves the spirit, the breath that sustains it. The very word in Arabic, *hubb* is closely related to the word for 'seed' (*habba*).

Ordinary-looking on the surface, the seed is the essential womb from which all else arises. Without the seed, there can be no root or branch, no leaf or fruit: no life, no continuation. So too, the essence and core of Islam is love for the Prophet ﷺ. Without it, there can be no true praxis of Islam, merely hollow mouthings and empty gestures. Love is the secret through which the religion has been transmitted over 1400 years: from master to pupil, parent to child, heart to heart.

But the seed exists hidden beneath the surface, in the soil of the heart. Whether it will grow or not depends greatly on the internal states of that heart, and on the external conditions that accompany it. Love does not grow within hearts of stone, and flowers that blossom in winter will perish from its chill. *Mawlid* – with its *qasa'id* and chanting, its remembrance and reflection – helps to soften and water hardened hearts, to warm the spiritual environment with the love of Rasulullah ﷺ and his lovers. It is the springtime of the soul, the season of sowing and blossoming. Rumi says:

> *You've been a rock for too long now*
> *Crumble yourself,*
> *And wild flowers will spring up at your feet*
> *Try something different:*
> *Surrender.*

The Autumn of Harvesting

The seed's function is to perpetuate itself: to produce fruits that are then harvested, ingested and enjoyed, that the seeds may become internalised and disseminated. For those whose hearts are already alive with the love of Rasulullah (s), who have become realised in perfection of faith, mawlid is an opportunity to taste the sweetness of the love's fruits, and to afford that sweetness to others. From its inception – and with very few notable exceptions – foremost among those arranging and partaking in mawlid have been the awliya-allah. As Ahmad bin Hanbal said, 'would you prevent them from enjoying an hour with their Lord?'

For lost, benighted souls like ourselves, this presents a golden opportunity. The fellowship of the awliya-allah is the single most effective, safest and fastest approach to love of Allah and his Rasul ﷺ to realisation of true faith – that this modern world provides. This is especially so when they are joyfully distributing the love of Rasulullah ﷺ to any and all who happen past. It is at these gatherings, filled not only with the love but the lovers of Rasulullah (s), that souls may become awakened to spiritual life. Mawlid is an opportunity to be imbued with beauty, and pruned of ugliness, at the hands of God's own gardeners.

Yet all of this is contingent. Rasulullah ﷺ said, *'actions are only by intentions,'* so we need to rectify and purify our intentions in order to truly attain benefit. My shaykh often says that, 'you get what you came for.' If we attend mawlid merely for entertainment, or for the food, such we shall receive.

If we attend to benefit, we surely shall. But if we attend sincerely desiring that – through the love of Rasulullah ﷺ, through the grace of the awliya-allah – Allah divest us of all that veils us from Him; then *wa Allahu yu`ti man ya sha'a bi-ghayri hisab*!

For this, we must learn to look beyond form to spirit, to go past means and attain ends. *Mawlid* is a means, not an end in-and-of itself. We are weary travellers on a long road; mawlid is a way-station – a place to refresh ourselves, to seek direction, to meet with friends, to pause and consider. But it is not the journey's end. *Oh wayfaring soul, struggling with yourself! Go home! And take me with you...*

May Allah allow us all to partake of the mawlid of Rasulullah (s), and to do so with the sincere intention of attaining love for him (s), through the blessedness and the grace of those who are his lovers. For within us, too, is a hidden seed, enduring the long dark winter of the heart; patiently waiting for the spring to come and awaken us all

◆⊰ THE SOLILOQUY OF THE FULL MOON ⊱◆

In this blessed month of the Prophet's  birth, this First Spring (*Rabi` al-Awwal*), may we all be awakened to light and love and life. And with Allah lies all taufiq. Peace and blessings upon His Messenger  and all those who follow him, every instant he is remembered by his lovers, and every instant the heedless forget.

TALIB AL-HABIB